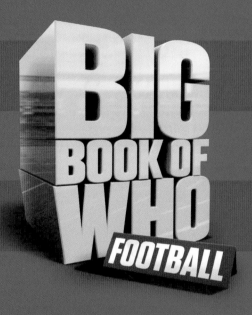

BIG
BOOK OF
WHO
FOOTBALL

Sports Illustrated Kids

Managing Editor and Publisher Bob Der
Creative Director Beth Power Bugler
Project Editor Andrea Woo
Director of Photography Marguerite Schropp Lucarelli

Created by 10Ten Media

Managing Director Scott Gramling
Creative Director Ian Knowles
Project Editor / Writer Joseph Levit
Senior Writer Tim Gramling
Staff Writers Steven Bennett, Zachary Cohen
Designer Elizabeth Flach
Reporter Corinne Cummings
Cover Illustration Artistic Image / AA Reps Inc.

Time Home Entertainment

Publisher Jim Childs
Vice President, Brand & Digital Strategy Steven Sandonato
Executive Director, Marketing Services Carol Pittard
Executive Director, Retail & Special Sales Tom Mifsud
Executive Publishing Director Joy Butts
Director, Bookazine Development & Marketing Laura Adam
Finance Director Glenn Buonocore
Associate Publishing Director Megan Pearlman
Assistant General Counsel Helen Wan
Assistant Director, Special Sales Ilene Schreider
Senior Book Production Manager Susan Chodakiewicz
Design & Prepress Manager Anne-Michelle Gallero
Brand Manager Jonathan White
Associate Prepress Manager Alex Voznesenskiy
Assistant Brand Manager Stephanie Braga

Editorial Director Stephen Koepp

Special thanks: Katherine Barnet, Jeremy Biloon, Rose Cirrincione, Jacqueline Fitzgerald, Christine Font, Jenna Goldberg, Hillary Hirsch, David Kahn, Amy Mangus, Kimberly Marshall, Amy Migliaccio, Nina Mistry, Dave Rozzelle, Ricardo Santiago, Adriana Tierno, Vanessa Wu

Welcome

Football is a game of stars. Quarterbacks who complete long passes with pinpoint accuracy, running backs with lightning-quick feet, and defensive stars with the strength to shed blocks before making tackles all help make the NFL the nation's most popular and exciting pro sports league. This book answers questions about many of the game's best players, both past and present, from all 32 NFL teams. We hope you enjoy it as much as the game itself!

Contents

3

CHAM

The players who achieved football's ultimate

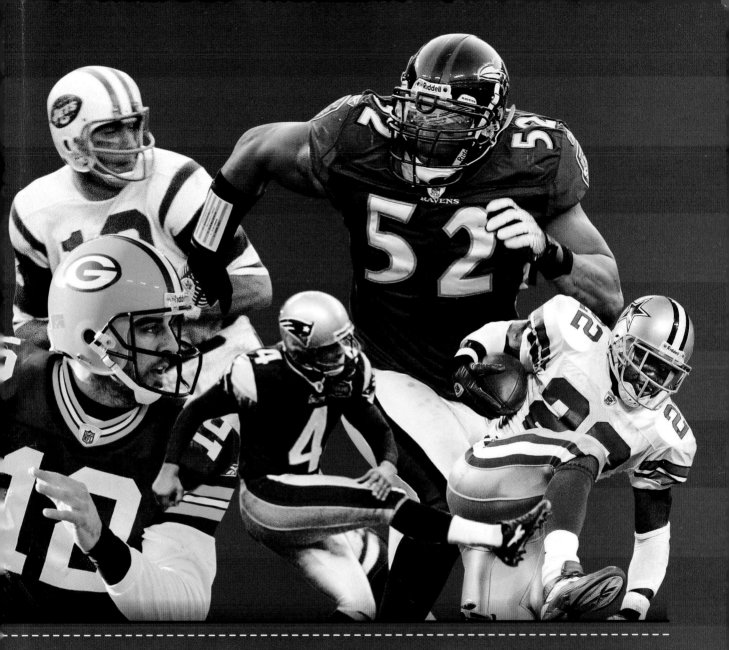

PIONS
prize, many of them more than once

Who was the MVP in the Saints' only Super Bowl appearance?

On February 7, 2010, *Drew Brees* led the New Orleans Saints to a 31–17 victory over the Indianapolis Colts in Super Bowl XLIV. He completed 32 of 39 passes for 228 yards and two touchdowns, and was named the game's most valuable player.

The Saints' Super Bowl was very special to New Orleans fans who had endured many losing seasons — the Saints failed to have a winning record in any of the first 20 years they existed! When Hurricane Katrina devastated the city in August 2005, it seemed New Orleans would never have an NFL champion. That's because the team's home stadium, the Louisiana Superdome, suffered so much damage in the storm that many people thought the Saints would have to permanently move to another city.

The Superdome was repaired before the 2006 season, just in time for Brees's first game as a Saint. That season, he led New Orleans to a playoff win, just the second in the history of the franchise. Three seasons later, the city of New Orleans finally had a Super Bowl champion!

Super Stat:

13

The NFL record number of times Brees passed for 300 or more yards in a game during the 2011 season

DID YOU KNOW?

FAST FACT: Drew Brees was selected by voters to appear on the cover of EA Sports' *Madden NFL 11* video game.

The Saints joined the NFL in 1967, but they won only one playoff game in 39 seasons before Drew Brees became the team's quarterback. New Orleans played in the first Super Bowl in the history of the franchise in 2010. That left only these four NFL teams to have never played in a Super Bowl:

Cleveland
Browns

Detroit
Lions

Houston
Texans

Jacksonville
Jaguars

Who was the first player to be named Super Bowl MVP?

Green Bay Packers quarterback *Bart Starr* is the original Super Bowl hero. He won MVP honors in each of the first two Super Bowls. The Packers won both games easily, but the road to the second title wasn't so simple. In the 1967 National Football League Championship game, Starr led Green Bay to a last-minute, come-from-behind, 21–17 win over the Dallas Cowboys. "The Ice Bowl" was one of the coldest games ever played (minus-45 wind chill temperatures). The weather was so brutal that one official's whistle froze to his lip!

FAST FACT: Eli Manning set several school records in college at Ole Miss, including overtaking his dad, Archie, in career touchdown passes. Eli threw for 81 scores, 50 more than his father.

Who is the only Giants player to win two Super Bowl MVP Awards?

Eli Manning was the MVP of Super Bowls XLII and XLVI. Both games were come-from-behind wins over the New England Patriots. And both featured remarkable completions to keep game-winning drives alive.

Trailing by four points on his final possession of Super Bowl XLII, in February 2008, Manning escaped the clutches of two Patriots, and launched a pass downfield. Seldom-used receiver David Tyree made a remarkable jumping catch, pinning the ball to his helmet with one hand while falling to the ground. Four years later, Manning completed a deep ball along the sidelines to Mario Manningham, who caught it in between two defenders and deftly touched his feet inbounds. Both plays helped lead to Giants wins.

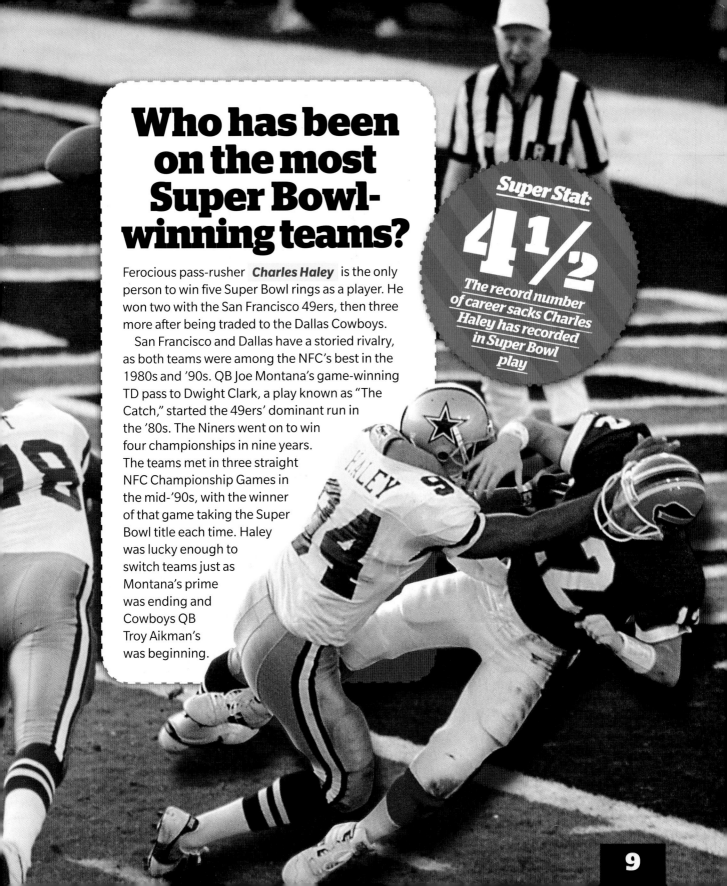

Who has been on the most Super Bowl-winning teams?

Ferocious pass-rusher *Charles Haley* is the only person to win five Super Bowl rings as a player. He won two with the San Francisco 49ers, then three more after being traded to the Dallas Cowboys.

San Francisco and Dallas have a storied rivalry, as both teams were among the NFC's best in the 1980s and '90s. QB Joe Montana's game-winning TD pass to Dwight Clark, a play known as "The Catch," started the 49ers' dominant run in the '80s. The Niners went on to win four championships in nine years. The teams met in three straight NFC Championship Games in the mid-'90s, with the winner of that game taking the Super Bowl title each time. Haley was lucky enough to switch teams just as Montana's prime was ending and Cowboys QB Troy Aikman's was beginning.

Super Stat:

4 1/2

The record number of career sacks Charles Haley has recorded in Super Bowl play

9

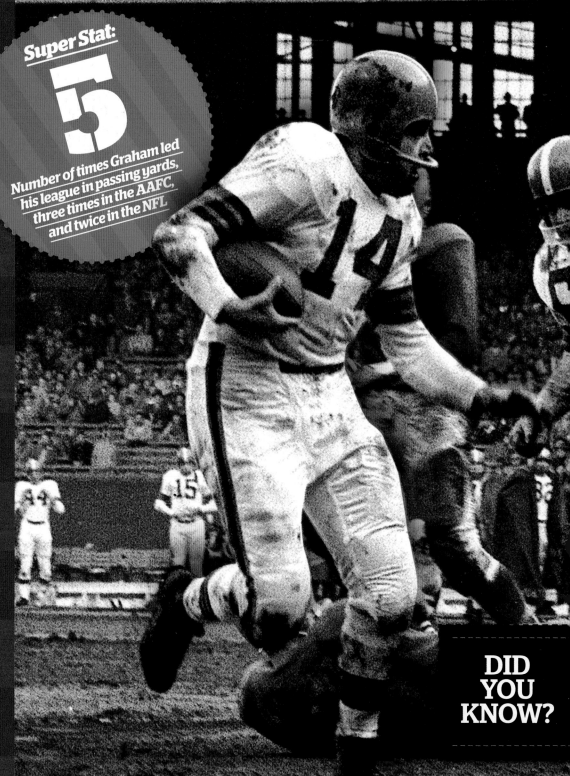

AT BAT   VISITORS   H   E

OUT INN.   CLEVELAND   H   E

Super Stat:

5

Number of times Graham led his league in passing yards, three times in the AAFC, and twice in the NFL

DID YOU KNOW?

FAST FACT: Otto Graham spent a season in the National Basketball League (now the NBA) before signing with the Cleveland Browns. His Rochester Royals won the NBL championship in 1946.

Who has the best winning percentage in NFL history as a quarterback?

In his 10-year pro football career, *Otto Graham* led the Cleveland Browns to a 114–20–4 record and played in his league's title game every season! Cleveland won all four All-American Football Conference (AAFC) championships before the league merged with the NFL in 1950. Many expected the Browns to struggle once they moved to the NFL, but they won the title that season and twice more before Graham retired. Cleveland went 57–13–1 over the six seasons Graham quarterbacked them in the NFL. His winning percentage of 81.4 is a league record.

The Browns lost three close title games in the only years that Graham failed to lead the team to its league's championship. He won three NFL MVP awards in addition to an AAFC MVP and an AAFC co-MVP. Graham's career average of 8.98 yards per pass attempt remains the highest mark in NFL history.

The Browns were named in 1946 after their first head coach, Paul Brown, who at the time was considered a young football genius. Brown had led nearby Ohio State University to a college football national title in 1942. Known as "The Father of Modern Football," the Hall of Fame coach set lasting trends in the sport with a number of innovations. Among them were using playbooks, introducing the concept of film study, and coming up with the idea to put a radio receiver in the quarterback's helmet so that coaches could talk to the player when he was on the field.

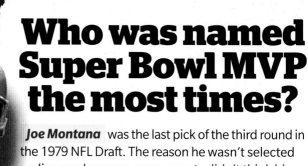

Who was named Super Bowl MVP the most times?

Joe Montana was the last pick of the third round in the 1979 NFL Draft. The reason he wasn't selected earlier was because many scouts didn't think his arm was as strong as most NFL quarterbacks. The San Francisco 49ers were lucky to grab Montana when they did. That's because he would go on to become the greatest Super Bowl quarterback in NFL history.

Montana led the 49ers to four Super Bowl victories, and he was named Super Bowl MVP three times. Not only could he make accurate throws, but his calm demeanor in high-pressure situations earned him the nickname "Joe Cool." One time that Montana used his cool was in Super Bowl XXIII against the Cincinnati Bengals. Down 16–13, the 49ers had the ball on their 8-yard line with 3:20 left in the fourth quarter. In the huddle, Montana pretended to spot comedian John Candy in the stands. This lightened the mood and helped the Niners go on a game-winning 92-yard drive. Montana always knew what to do when it mattered most.

Super Stat:

122

Super Bowl passes thrown by Montana without an interception; all other Super Bowl quarterbacks to have thrown 50 or more passes have at least one interception

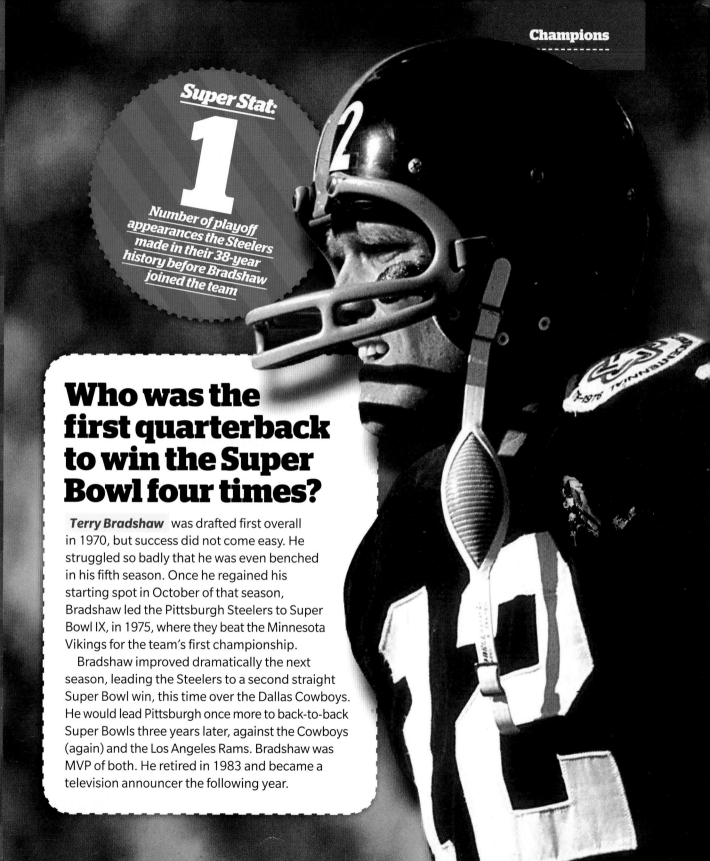

Super Stat:

1

Number of playoff appearances the Steelers made in their 38-year history before Bradshaw joined the team

Who was the first quarterback to win the Super Bowl four times?

Terry Bradshaw was drafted first overall in 1970, but success did not come easy. He struggled so badly that he was even benched in his fifth season. Once he regained his starting spot in October of that season, Bradshaw led the Pittsburgh Steelers to Super Bowl IX, in 1975, where they beat the Minnesota Vikings for the team's first championship.

Bradshaw improved dramatically the next season, leading the Steelers to a second straight Super Bowl win, this time over the Dallas Cowboys. He would lead Pittsburgh once more to back-to-back Super Bowls three years later, against the Cowboys (again) and the Los Angeles Rams. Bradshaw was MVP of both. He retired in 1983 and became a television announcer the following year.

Who was MVP the last time the Packers won the Super Bowl?

Even though *Aaron Rodgers* was selected in the first round of the 2005 NFL Draft, he knew he would have to wait a while before he got a chance to be the Green Bay Packers' starting quarterback. That's because the Packers had legendary quarterback Brett Favre as their starter. Favre was a three-time winner of the NFL's MVP award, and the most popular player among Green Bay's fans. Sure enough, Rodgers would end up throwing a total of only 59 passes over his first three seasons with Green Bay.

Rodgers finally got his chance to be the Packers' starting quarterback in 2008, after Favre left the team and joined the New York Jets. When Green Bay slipped from a 13–3 record in 2007 to a 6–10 record in '08 in Rodgers's first season as the team's quarterback, the Packers seemed to be an awfully long way from reaching a Super Bowl.

However, Rodgers would soon turn the team around. He guided Green Bay to an 11–5 record in 2009. The following year, the Packers made it all the way to Super Bowl XLV to face the Pittsburgh Steelers. Rodgers would end up leading Green Bay to a 31–26 victory. He was named Super Bowl MVP after completing 24 of 39 passes for 304 yards and three touchdowns with no interceptions. Both Rodgers and Packers fans certainly agreed that his late arrival as the team's starting quarterback was well worth the wait!

DID YOU KNOW?

FAST FACT: December 12, 2012, (or 12/12/12) was recognized in the state of Wisconsin as "Aaron Rodgers Day." The Green Bay quarterback wears the Number 12.

Prior to the 2005 NFL Draft, Rodgers was talked about being the No. 1 overall pick. The San Francisco 49ers, who were selecting first, seemed like a perfect match. They needed a quarterback, and Rodgers had become a star just across San Francisco Bay, at the University of California, in Berkeley. But the 49ers instead drafted University of Utah quarterback Alex Smith. Rodgers was asked by a reporter how disappointed he was about dropping to the 24th pick. "Not as disappointed as the 49ers will be that they didn't draft me," Rodgers said.

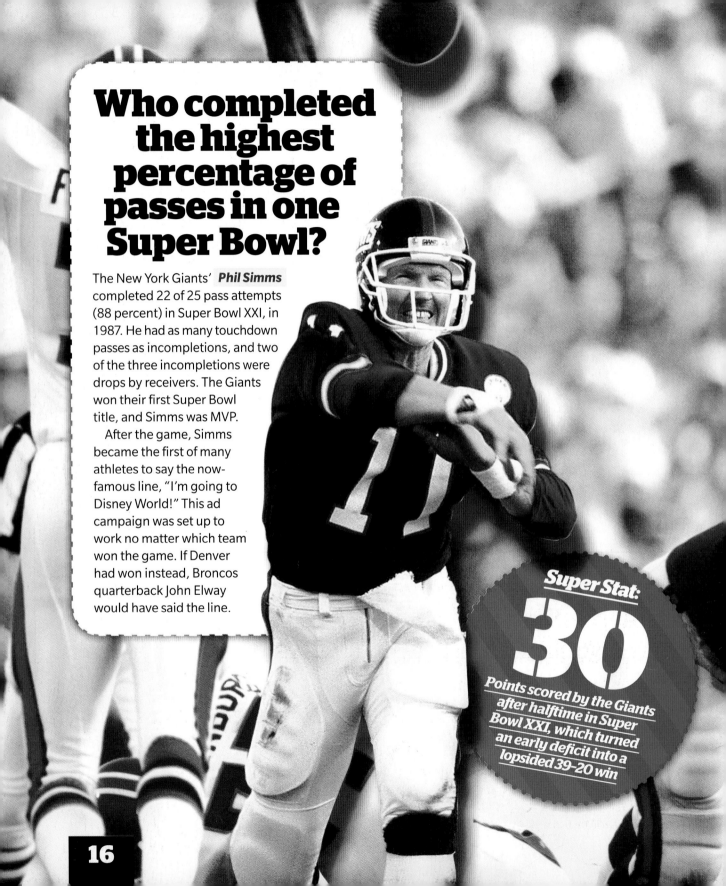

Who completed the highest percentage of passes in one Super Bowl?

The New York Giants' *Phil Simms* completed 22 of 25 pass attempts (88 percent) in Super Bowl XXI, in 1987. He had as many touchdown passes as incompletions, and two of the three incompletions were drops by receivers. The Giants won their first Super Bowl title, and Simms was MVP.

After the game, Simms became the first of many athletes to say the now-famous line, "I'm going to Disney World!" This ad campaign was set up to work no matter which team won the game. If Denver had won instead, Broncos quarterback John Elway would have said the line.

Super Stat:

30

Points scored by the Giants after halftime in Super Bowl XXI, which turned an early deficit into a lopsided 39–20 win

> **FAST FACT: Emmitt Smith carried the ball more often (4,409 attempts) for more yards (18,355 yards) and more touchdowns (164) than any other running back in NFL history.**

Who has rushed for the most career touchdowns in Super Bowl history?

The Dallas Cowboys beat the Pittsburgh Steelers, 27–17, in Super Bowl XXX, in January 1996. The Cowboys became the first team to win three Super Bowls in a four-year span. And it was the legs of a running back named *Emmitt Smith* that helped carry them there.

Smith's two touchdowns against the Steelers were the fourth and fifth Super Bowl rushing touchdowns of his career, the most ever. He scored at least once in all three Super Bowls in which he played. Smith found the end zone when it mattered most: All five of his Super Bowl touchdowns came in the second half of games.

Who has the most rushing TDs in one Super Bowl?

Terrell Davis suffered a blinding migraine headache that kept the running back on the Denver Broncos' sideline for almost the entire second quarter of Super Bowl XXXII, in 1998. Thanks to emergency treatment on the sideline, Davis was able to return for the second half and wound up rushing for 157 yards and a Super Bowl-record three touchdowns in his team's 31–24 win over the Green Bay Packers. It was Denver's first victory in five trips to the Super Bowl.

17

FAST FACT: John Elway retired a few months after being named MVP of Super Bowl XXXIII. He is the only player to retire as the reigning Super Bowl MVP.

Who is the oldest quarterback to lead his team to victory in the Super Bowl?

I t seemed as if *John Elway* would never win a Super Bowl. His Denver Broncos lost football's biggest game three times while Elway was in his 20s, and each defeat was by more points than the previous time: The Broncos lost by 19 points to the New York Giants in 1987, by 32 points to the Washington Redskins in 1988, then by 45 points to the San Francisco 49ers in 1990.

Elway was 37 when he tore a tendon in his throwing arm during the 1997 NFL pre-season. He refused to let the injury slow him down. Elway went on to play every game that season, and he led the Broncos to Super Bowl XXXII to face the favored defending champion Green Bay Packers. The Broncos upset the Packers, 31–24, as Elway became the oldest quarterback to win the Super Bowl. He would break his own record the following year when, as a 38-year-old, he beat the Atlanta Falcons in Super Bowl XXXIII. Elway was named MVP of Denver's 34–19 victory.

DID YOU KNOW?

John Elway played football and baseball in college at Stanford. He batted .318 for the minor-league Oneonta Yankees in 1982 after New York selected him in the 1981 Major League Baseball draft.

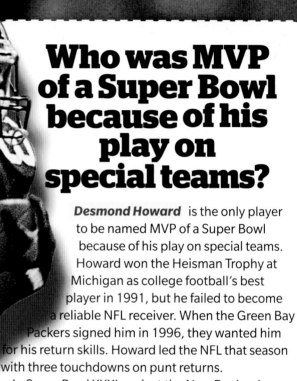

Who was MVP of a Super Bowl because of his play on special teams?

Desmond Howard is the only player to be named MVP of a Super Bowl because of his play on special teams. Howard won the Heisman Trophy at Michigan as college football's best player in 1991, but he failed to become a reliable NFL receiver. When the Green Bay Packers signed him in 1996, they wanted him for his return skills. Howard led the NFL that season with three touchdowns on punt returns.

In Super Bowl XXXI against the New England Patriots, he had two long punt returns in the first half to set up Green Bay scores. And right after the Patriots scored to start a second-half comeback, Howard's 99-yard kickoff return for a touchdown shifted momentum back to Green Bay. It turned out to be the game's final score. And it solidified Howard's place as one of the best return men in NFL history.

Super Stat:

875

Record number of yards Howard gained on punt returns in 1996, which is a single-season NFL record

Super Stat:

78

Number of yards the Steelers gained in 2:02 on their game-winning drive in the fourth quarter of Super Bowl XLIII

Who is the last wide receiver to be named MVP of a Super Bowl?

In one of the most exciting Super Bowls ever, *Santonio Holmes* made an acrobatic catch in the end zone with 35 seconds remaining in the fourth quarter of Super Bowl XLIII, in 2009. The catch was Holmes's ninth of the game and helped him earn MVP honors in the Pittsburgh Steelers' 27–23 win.

The Steelers led the Arizona Cardinals after three quarters and seemed poised to win. But Arizona's star wide receiver, Larry Fitzgerald, scored two fourth-quarter touchdowns to give the Cardinals a three-point lead with less than three minutes remaining. The Steelers started their final drive at their own 22-yard line, and they quickly moved the ball downfield. On the final play of the drive, Holmes grabbed the touchdown with his feet barely inbounds to secure the win.

FAST FACT: Joe Flacco is the only quarterback in NFL history to win at least one playoff game in each of his first five pro seasons.

Super Stat:

11

Number of touchdown passes Flacco threw during the playoffs that followed the 2012 season, which tied Joe Montana for most TDs without an interception in one postseason

Who was MVP the last time the Ravens reached the Super Bowl?

The playoffs following the 2012 NFL regular season were one big *Joe Flacco* party. After his Baltimore Ravens beat the Indianapolis Colts, he led his team to Denver to face the AFC's top-seeded Broncos. That's where Flacco completed a game-tying 70-yard touchdown pass to Jacoby Jones with less than a minute remaining in the fourth quarter. The play became known as the "Flacco Fling."

The Ravens went on to beat the Broncos in overtime, then upset the New England Patriots the following week in the AFC Championship Game. Two weeks later, Flacco faced the San Francisco 49ers in Super Bowl XLVII. He built a 21–3 lead with three touchdown passes in the first half, and would finish the game with 287 passing yards. His ability to avoid throwing an interception helped secure the 34–31 win and MVP honors.

DID YOU KNOW?

Flacco is the oldest of six children — five boys and one girl — from a very athletic family. His brother Mike was selected by the Baltimore Orioles in the 2009 Major League Baseball Draft, and his brother John is a wide receiver at Stanford University. Sister Stephanie was a field hockey and basketball star in high school.

Who has kicked the most Super Bowl-winning field goals?

No Super Bowl has ever gone to overtime, but Super Bowl XXXVI, in February 2002, came close. After the St. Louis Rams tied the game late in the fourth quarter, the New England Patriots drove to set up an **Adam Vinatieri** field goal try. Vinatieri made the 48-yard kick as time expired to become the first player to score on a Super Bowl's final play. Two years later, he made a 41-yard field goal with four seconds left to beat the Carolina Panthers in the Super Bowl and become known as "Mr. Clutch"!

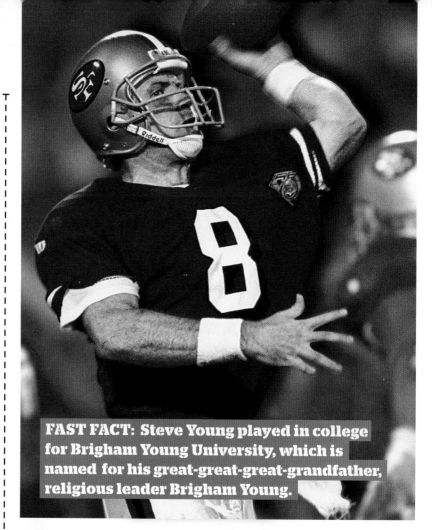

FAST FACT: Steve Young played in college for Brigham Young University, which is named for his great-great-great-grandfather, religious leader Brigham Young.

Who has thrown the most touchdown passes in one Super Bowl?

Steve Young overcame a career of frustration when he set a Super Bowl record with six TD passes to help the San Francisco 49ers crush the San Diego Chargers, 49–26, in Super Bowl XXIX, in January 1995. After having started his career with just three wins in two seasons with the Tampa Bay Buccaneers, Young was traded to San Francisco. He then spent four years backing up the great Joe Montana.

Even after taking over for Montana, Young lost two straight NFC Championship games to the Dallas Cowboys. But he broke through the following year by beating the Cowboys in the Championship game, and then the Chargers in the Super Bowl.

Who has scored the longest touchdown by a defensive player in a Super Bowl?

The Pittsburgh Steelers' **James Harrison** returned an interception 100 yards for a key score in Super Bowl XLIII, in Feburary 2009. When the Arizona Cardinals had the ball on the Steelers' 1-yard line late in the first half, Harrison crept up toward the line, and the Cards assumed he'd be blitzing. Instead, Harrison faked a blitz and backpedaled in front of the intended target — receiver Anquan Boldin. Harrison caught the pass on his goal line and took off down the right sideline.

Harrison was tackled by Larry Fitzgerald just as he reached his 100th yard, scoring as time expired in the first half. While chasing him, Fitzgerald had run into his own teammate, preventing Fitzgerald from making the tackle earlier in the play. An exhausted Harrison lay on the ground in the end zone for a while, then returned to the bench and immediately used an oxygen mask to regain his breath!

Super Stat:

16

Number of sacks Harrison recorded in 2008, the most ever by a Steelers player in one season

Who has the most career passing yards in Super Bowl history?

It took *Tom Brady* a lot of determination and luck to crack the New England Patriots' starting lineup, but he's been a star ever since. Brady was the MVP of Super Bowl victories over the St. Louis Rams and Carolina Panthers, and he won a third Super Bowl against the Philadelphia Eagles, in February 2005. Since then, the Patriots have lost two close contests in the NFL title game, both times to the New York Giants. In those five Super Bowls, Brady has thrown for a record 1,277 yards.

Brady wasn't much of a star in college at the University of Michigan. As a senior, he even had to share his quarterback job with highly touted teammate Drew Henson. At the 2000 NFL Draft, six quarterbacks were selected ahead of Brady, who wasn't taken until the sixth round. He got his first chance to start when Patriots quarterback Drew Bledsoe suffered an injury in September 2001. Brady promptly led New England to the first Super Bowl title in franchise history.

Super Stat:

50

Number of touchdown passes Brady threw in 2007, the most ever by an NFL quarterback in one season

DID YOU KNOW?

FAST FACT: Brady played catcher for his high school's baseball team and was selected in the 18th round of the 1995 Major League Baseball Draft by the Montreal Expos. (The Expos moved to Washington in 2004 and became the Nationals.)

Bill Belichick, who became head coach of the New England Patriots the same year the team drafted Tom Brady (2000), was once the head coach of the New York Jets . . . for *one day*! Belichick ended up giving a resignation speech at the press conference that had been scheduled to announce his hiring. Although the Patriots were later forced to give the Jets a first-round draft pick as compensation, New England got the better of the deal. Brady and Belichick have more wins than any quarterback-coach duo in NFL history.

Who quarterbacked the team that pulled off the biggest Super Bowl upset?

Joe Namath led the New York Jets to a shocking 16–7 win over the Baltimore Colts in Super Bowl III, in January 1969. Few people expected the AFL's Jets to win. The NFL's Colts had lost one game all season and were coming off a 34–0 shutout of the Cleveland Browns. Namath, meanwhile, had thrown more interceptions than touchdowns that season. The NFL's Packers had also handily beaten the AFL entrant in the first two Super Bowls, so most people thought that proved the NFL's superiority to the AFL. Despite these facts, Namath famously guaranteed a Jets upset victory, making headlines and enraging his coach. It was Namath, however, who had the last laugh.

Super Stat:

18

Number of points by which oddsmakers had favored the Colts over the Jets prior to Super Bowl III

Super Stat:

23

Number of points allowed by the Ravens over their four post-season games that followed the 2000 regular season

Who is the last linebacker to be named MVP of a Super Bowl?

The saying "defense wins championships" has never been more true than during the 2000 regular season, and the post-season that followed. Baltimore Ravens linebacker *Ray Lewis* was named Super Bowl MVP after recording three solo tackles, two assists, and four passes defended in a 34–7 win over the New York Giants in Super Bowl XXXV.

It was a fitting ending to a season in which the Ravens were historically strong against the run, allowing opponents to average only 60.6 rushing yards per game. Baltimore's mediocre offense went five straight games without a TD, yet the Ravens still won their last 11 games. Lewis was also named NFL Defensive Player of the Year.

PERSON

Men who are known for more than just

ALITIES

the way they play the game on the field

Who is the running back known as "MoJo"?

In the 2006 NFL Draft, all 32 teams passed on their chance to select *Maurice Jones-Drew* in the first round. Although Jones-Drew had displayed a lot of talent in college at UCLA, most teams felt he was too short to succeed in the pros. That didn't sit well with the 5' 7" running back. After he was drafted by the Jacksonville Jaguars late in the second round, he chose to wear the Number 32 on his jersey as motivation. "Mojo," as he's often called, wanted to show those 32 teams (including his own) what they had passed up.

Though short by NFL standards, Jones-Drew is sturdy, quick, and strong. He also has terrific balance. It took some time for him to get an opportunity to show off all of his talents. Veteran Fred Taylor was the Jaguars' starting running back during Jones-Drew's first three seasons with the team. MoJo became the starter after Taylor joined the New England Patriots in 2009, which was the first of three straight seasons of more than 1,300 rushing yards for Jones-Drew. His 1,606 rushing yards in 2011 led the NFL. It was quite the output from someone scouts thought wouldn't be able to measure up.

DID YOU KNOW?

FAST FACT: Maurice Jones-Drew had a torn meniscus in his left knee for all 14 games he played in 2010.

Maurice Jones-Drew might be one of the NFL's shortest players at 5' 7", but he's not *the* shortest. In fact, he's not even the league's shortest running back, a distinction that goes to 5' 6" Darren Sproles of the New Orleans Saints. The shortest player in the league in 2012 was 5' 5" Trindon Holliday of the Denver Broncos, who that season led the NFL in punt return yards with 481. Holliday raised his game another notch in the playoffs, scoring against the Baltimore Ravens on the longest punt return for a touchdown (90 yards) in NFL post-season history.

Who was the leader of the "New York Sack Exchange" of the 1980s Jets?

The New York Jets' dominant mid-1980s defensive line — Joe Klecko, Marty Lyons, Abdul Salaam, and **Mark Gastineau** — formed the New York Sack Exchange. They got their name after ringing the opening bell at the New York Stock Exchange in 1981, but they *earned* the name by chasing down quaterbacks. Gastineau led the NFL in sacks with 19 in 1983. He then set an NFL single-season record with 22 in 1984. The record stood until the New York Giants' Michael Strahan tallied 22½ in 2001.

FAST FACT: Boomer Esiason won the NFL MVP award in 1988.

Who was the NFL quarterback known as "Boomer"?

Sometimes, people get nicknames early in life. Such was the case for *Norman "Boomer" Esiason*. While his mother was still pregnant with him, his father felt her belly and was surprised by the power he felt. "He must be a boomer because he kicks so much," Esiason's father said. But becoming a kicker was not in the cards for Boomer.

Instead, Esiason ended up throwing passes as a star quarterback. He was best known for his mastery of Cincinnati Bengals head coach Sam Wyche's no-huddle offense. The team rode that offense all the way to Super Bowl XXIII, in January 1989, which the Bengals narrowly lost, 20–16, to the San Francisco 49ers.

Who is the former NFL running back known as "The Bus"?

According to **_Jerome Bettis_**, he got his nickname during his college days at Notre Dame. But Pittsburgh radio commentator Myron Cope popularized it when he began calling Bettis "The Bus" during the broadcast of a Steelers game against the Green Bay Packers in 1998. Bettis kept dragging defenders for several yards after contact, as if they were riding a bus.

Bettis carried many players into the end zone with him during a successful career. He was drafted by the Los Angeles Rams in 1993, and went out a champion with the Super Bowl-winning Steelers in February 2006.

Who was forced to change the way he celebrates a sack?

Wide receivers are better known for celebrating big plays in quirky ways than players at any other NFL position. But they aren't the only players who do so. Many defensive linemen and linebackers perform distinctive gestures after tackling a running back for a loss or sacking a quarterback. While NFL officials don't penalize all such moves, the league did make a decision in 2010 to end the celebration that Minnesota Vikings defensive end *Jared Allen* would perform. Allen's move was to drop to one knee after a sack, and then act as if he had just lassoed the quarterback. He would complete the rodeo move by pretending to tie up the legs of a calf.

In order to cut down on celebrations that called attention to the accomplishments of an individual player rather than his team, the NFL ruled that celebrations would be penalized when they were on the ground. Since Allen's knee would touch the turf, it constituted a 15-yard penalty for excessive celebration. Allen has certainly had plenty of opportunities to celebrate: He has twice led the NFL in sacks, in 2007 with 15½, and in 2011 with 22.

Super Stat:

22

The number of sacks Allen tallied in 2011, which was one short of breaking Michael Strahan's NFL record for most sacks in one season

DID YOU KNOW?

FAST FACT: Jared Allen and Hall of Famer Reggie White are the only players in NFL history to record as many as 14½ sacks in three straight seasons.

Jared Allen has been credited with four safeties in his NFL career. That's tied for the most in NFL history with former Detroit Lions defensive tackle Doug English and former linebacker Ted Hendricks, who played for three different teams during his 15 NFL.seasons, most of which were with the Oakland Raiders. Allen's fourth career safety came on December 4, 2011, against the Denver Broncos. On the Broncos' first play from scrimmage, Allen tackled Denver running back Willis McGahee in the end zone.

Who was the NFL running back known as "Sweetness"?

Walter Payton of the Chicago Bears was called Sweetness, but no one is certain why. While some say it was his grace on the field, others cite his easygoing personality off it. The name could be ironic, since Payton was aggressive on the field, often dishing out as much punishment as he took.

For all the wear and tear, Payton was remarkably durable. His 170 consecutive starts between 1975 and '87 are the most ever for a running back. Payton was a two-time NFL MVP who owned many big records when he retired. Emmitt Smith broke his career rushing record of 16,726 yards. Corey Dillon first broke his single-game mark of 275 rushing yards. And Jerry Rice broke Payton's record of 21,264 career yards from scrimmage.

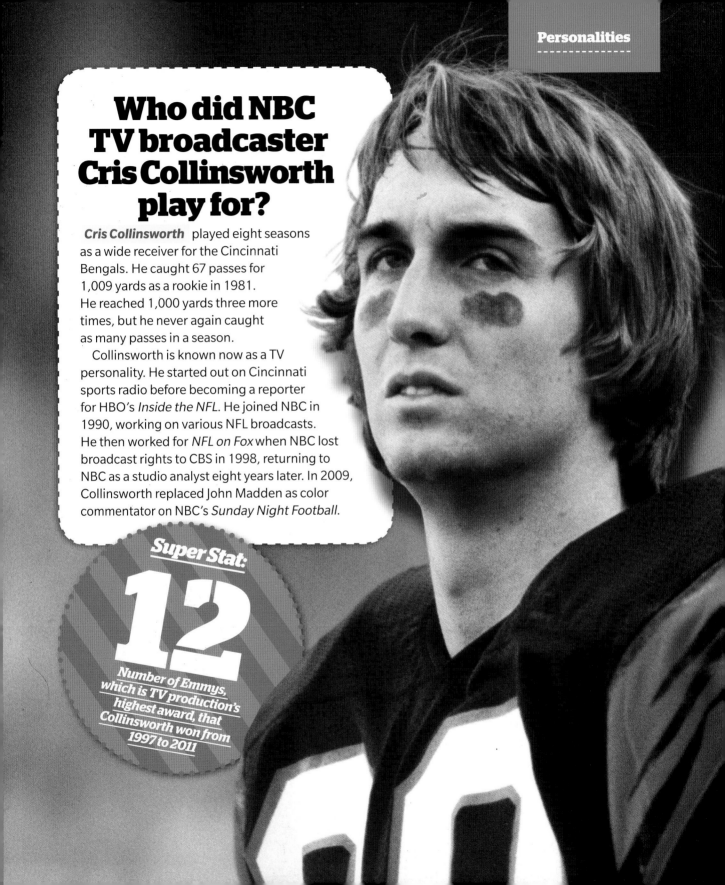

Who did NBC TV broadcaster Cris Collinsworth play for?

Cris Collinsworth played eight seasons as a wide receiver for the Cincinnati Bengals. He caught 67 passes for 1,009 yards as a rookie in 1981. He reached 1,000 yards three more times, but he never again caught as many passes in a season.

Collinsworth is known now as a TV personality. He started out on Cincinnati sports radio before becoming a reporter for HBO's *Inside the NFL*. He joined NBC in 1990, working on various NFL broadcasts. He then worked for *NFL on Fox* when NBC lost broadcast rights to CBS in 1998, returning to NBC as a studio analyst eight years later. In 2009, Collinsworth replaced John Madden as color commentator on NBC's *Sunday Night Football*.

Super Stat:

12

Number of Emmys, which is TV production's highest award, that Collinsworth won from 1997 to 2011

FAST FACT: Deion Sanders is the only athlete to play in both a Super Bowl and a World Series.

DID YOU KNOW?

Super Stat:

6

The number of ways Sanders scored NFL touchdowns: rushing and receiving, and on returns of a fumble, interception, kickoff, and punt

Who is known as "Prime Time"?

Deion Sanders was a larger-than-life personality. He was known for brash statements about his outstanding abilities, but he backed it up with excellent play on the field. Sanders's trademark move was the high-step, which he performed as he neared the end zone. He would put one hand behind his head and hold the football outstretched in his other as he pranced toward the goal line.

Sanders was labeled "Prime Time" in high school after showcasing his basketball moves in pick-up games played during the prime-time TV hours. He lived up to the name during a 14-year NFL career in which he played for five teams: the Atlanta Falcons, San Francisco 49ers, Dallas Cowboys, Washington Redskins, and Baltimore Ravens. His 1,331 career yards on interception returns ranks fourth in NFL history, and his nine touchdowns on interception returns is tied for fourth. Sanders won Super Bowls with the 49ers and Cowboys. And in 2011, he was inducted into the Pro Football Hall of Fame.

Deion Sanders was such a great athlete that he played Major League Baseball during the same time that he played in the NFL. He suited up for the four teams shown here over nine big league seasons. His best season was 1992, when he hit .304 with 14 triples and 26 steals for the Atlanta Braves.

New York Yankees

Atlanta Braves

Cincinnati Reds

San Francisco Giants

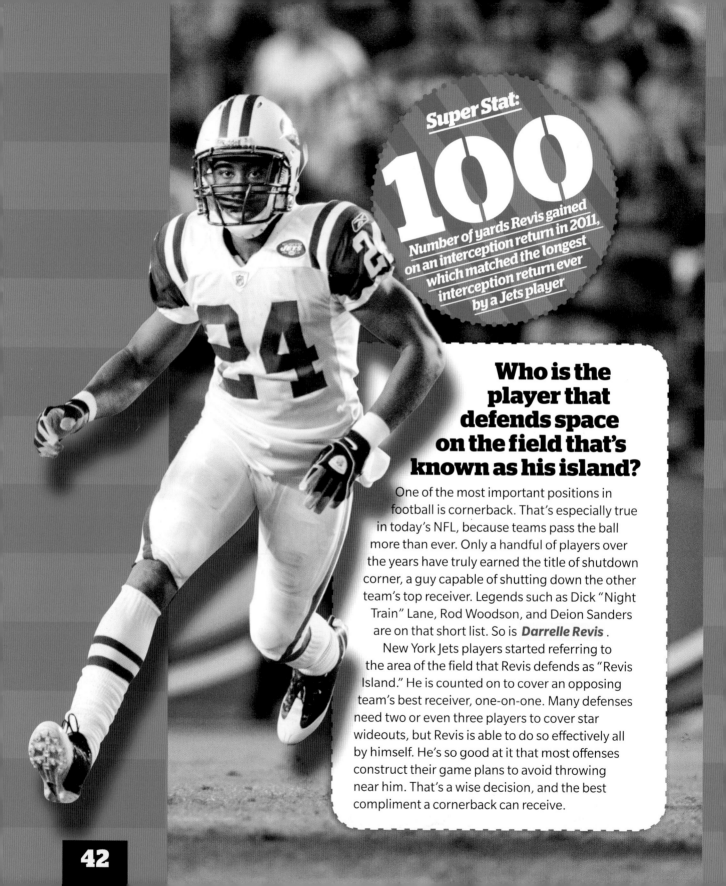

100

Number of yards Revis gained on an interception return in 2011, which matched the longest interception return ever by a Jets player

Who is the player that defends space on the field that's known as his island?

One of the most important positions in football is cornerback. That's especially true in today's NFL, because teams pass the ball more than ever. Only a handful of players over the years have truly earned the title of shutdown corner, a guy capable of shutting down the other team's top receiver. Legends such as Dick "Night Train" Lane, Rod Woodson, and Deion Sanders are on that short list. So is *Darrelle Revis* .

New York Jets players started referring to the area of the field that Revis defends as "Revis Island." He is counted on to cover an opposing team's best receiver, one-on-one. Many defenses need two or even three players to cover star wideouts, but Revis is able to do so effectively all by himself. He's so good at it that most offenses construct their game plans to avoid throwing near him. That's a wise decision, and the best compliment a cornerback can receive.

Who is known for the wackiest end zone celebrations?

Many wide receivers put on an act after scoring a touchdown, but *Terrell Owens* tops them all. In a game against the Baltimore Ravens in 2004, Owens scored for the Philadelphia Eagles, then made fun of Ray Lewis by mocking the linebacker's pre-game dance. During a game in Dallas in 2000, he twice sprinted after scores to celebrate on the Cowboys' star logo. The second time he did it, Dallas safety George Teague ran after him and knocked Owens down at midfield, which started a heated confrontation between players from each team.

Owens has a silly side, too. He once laid down in the end zone after a touchdown and pretended to nap, using the football as a pillow. Another time, he threw popcorn in his face after reaching the end zone. He even once celebrated by borrowing a cheerleader's pompoms before doing a little dance. *Hooray!*

Super Stat:

153

Number of career TD passes Owens has caught, the NFL's third-highest total of all time behind Jerry Rice and Randy Moss

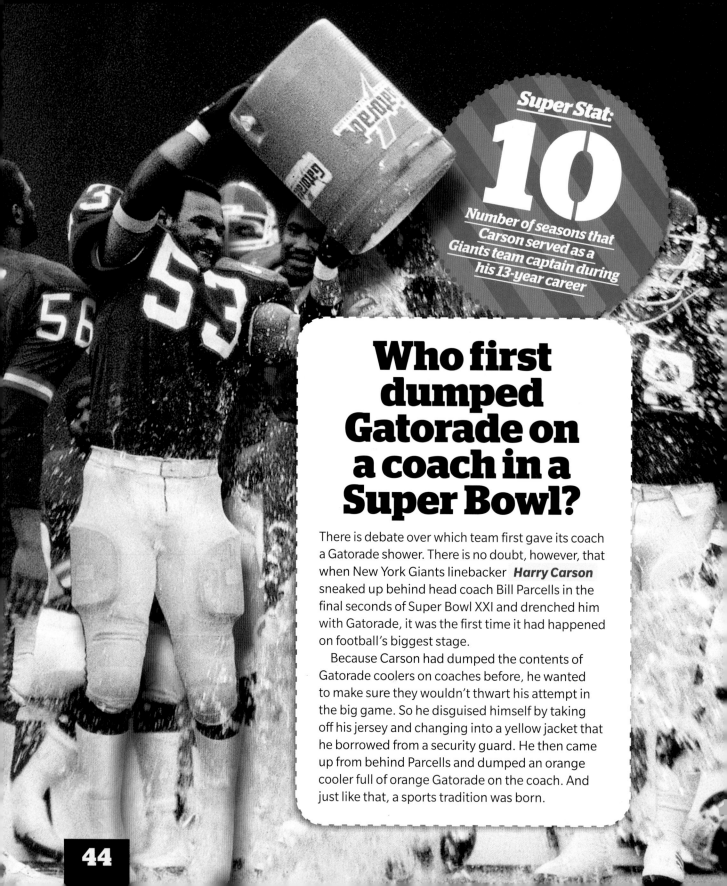

Who first dumped Gatorade on a coach in a Super Bowl?

There is debate over which team first gave its coach a Gatorade shower. There is no doubt, however, that when New York Giants linebacker *Harry Carson* sneaked up behind head coach Bill Parcells in the final seconds of Super Bowl XXI and drenched him with Gatorade, it was the first time it had happened on football's biggest stage.

Because Carson had dumped the contents of Gatorade coolers on coaches before, he wanted to make sure they wouldn't thwart his attempt in the big game. So he disguised himself by taking off his jersey and changing into a yellow jacket that he borrowed from a security guard. He then came up from behind Parcells and dumped an orange cooler full of orange Gatorade on the coach. And just like that, a sports tradition was born.

FAST FACT: John Randle's 137½ career sacks are more than any other defensive tackle since sacks became an official NFL statistic in 1982.

Who has the wildest hairdo among NFL players?

Troy Polamalu of the Pittsburgh Steelers wins that honor. He claims he hasn't cut his hair in more than a decade! Polamalu showed off his long, curly mane in TV commercials for the shampoo brand Head & Shoulders. Hair that long can get you in trouble on the field, though. After Polamalu made an interception against Kansas City in 2006, Larry Johnson of the Chiefs pulled the Pittsburgh safety to the ground by his hair. That action is legal in the NFL. What wasn't legal was the way Johnson then pulled Polamalu back up by his hair. *Ouch!*

Who is known for wearing the craziest face paint?

Many NFL players wear eyeblack to reduce glare from the sun or stadium lights. But former Minnesota Vikings defensive tackle *John Randle* used it to increase the power of *his* glare. Randle would paint his face in an effort to intimidate offensive linemen and throw them off their games.

Randle, however, didn't rely on antics alone. He was a scary-good defender who worked hard to make up for a frame that was relatively small for a defensive lineman. Because he was only 6'1" and less than 250 pounds coming out of college, Randle wasn't even drafted by an NFL team. Yet he still went on to make the Pro Football Hall of Fame.

Who is known as "Run DMC"?

Oakland Raiders star running back *Darren McFadden* has a rare blend of speed and power. When he breaks into the open field or turns the corner on a defense, the play is a touchdown waiting to happen. From a statistical standpoint, McFadden has busted loose for some truly big days. In a 2010 game against the Denver Broncos, he broke loose for 165 yards and three touchdowns on 16 carries, with another score on a reception. In 2011, he buried the New York Jets with 171 yards and two touchdowns, including a 70-yard scoring scamper.

Unfortunately for the Raiders, McFadden was unable to stay healthy during the first five years of his NFL career. He started just 44 of a possible 80 pro games. Because of that missed time, he had a career yearly average of only 667 yards rushing per season through 2012.

As a rookie in 2008, McFadden injured his big toe, which limited his effectiveness for the next 14 games. The following season, a torn meniscus in his knee held him back. He rushed for more than 1,000 yards once during his first five seasons in the league. That happened in 2010, when he had to deal with a nagging hamstring injury. In 2011, he was leading the NFL in rushing after six weeks, with 610 yards. However, he suffered a sprained foot in the next game, and missed the rest of the season. In 2012, a sprained right ankle was the injury that held him in check.

If McFadden can ever stay healthy, NFL defenses had better watch out. Until then, the Raiders will continue to hope their star running back's luck finally starts to turn around.

Super Stat:

16

Number of touchdowns McFadden scored as a junior in college for the University of Arkansas Razorbacks

FAST FACT: In 2010, Darren McFadden became just the fourth Raiders player to total four touchdowns in one game. The others were Marcus Allen, Art Powell, and Harvey Williams.

DID YOU KNOW?

As a college star for the Arkansas Razorbacks, Darren McFadden became only the second player to twice win the Doak Walker Award, which is given each year to the nation's top running back. The other was Ricky Williams, who played in college for the Texas Longhorns.

Who once changed his name to match the number he wore?

Chad Johnson averaged nearly 80 catches per season over seven years with the Cincinnati Bengals. He was known just as well, however, for his antics *off* the field.

Before the 2008 season, Johnson legally changed his last name to Ochocinco. He did it to highlight a nickname he had created for himself based on his Number 85 jersey. In Spanish, *ocho* is the number eight and *cinco* is five. Regardless of what fans thought of Johnson's quirks, he certainly kept people entertained. He once outraced a horse for charity, and in 2011 he rode a 1,500-pound bull named Déjà Blue (for 1.5 seconds) in a professional bull riding event.

Super Stat:

65

Number of touchdown passes Johnson caught over 10 seasons with the Cincinnati Bengals, the most TD receptions in team history

Super Stat

20½

Number of sacks Watt had in 2012, only two fewer than the NFL record for most sacks in one season

Who is known as the "Mega-Watt"?

It is rare that an NFL player is so dominant that he forces opposing teams to change the way they prepare for a game. But that's exactly the kind of fear and respect that opposing coaching staffs have for Houston Texans defensive lineman **J.J. Watt**. His production in all phases of the game has led many to call him Mega-Watt.

Watt's signature move is leaping into the air to knock down a pass before it gets beyond the line of scrimmage. Not only did he lead all linemen with 16 passes defended in 2012, but no other NFL lineman had even as many as 10. Watt is so good at this skill that to prepare for a game against the Texans, New England Patriots head coach Bill Belichick had racquetball paddles held in front of quarterback Tom Brady in practice. Belichick wanted Brady to know how difficult it is to pass with Watt's hands in the way. Watt's ability to knock down passes impressed TV commentator Jon Gruden so much that Gruden gave Watt another nickname: J.J. Swatt.

Who is known as "The Red Rifle"?

A quarterback who can throw with velocity and accuracy can be said to have a rifle arm. Add in a red head of hair, and it's no surprise that people might call you The Red Rifle. That's what has happened for Cincinnati Bengals QB *Andy Dalton*. He doesn't mind the moniker, but Dalton does have a preference when it comes to his name: "Andy," he says. "Andy works. It's just Andy." No matter the name, in his first two NFL seasons, Dalton helped the team make its first back-to-back playoff appearances (2011 and 2012) since 1981 and 1982, nearly five years before Dalton was born!

FAST FACT: Greene is the only player to force a fumble, recover a fumble, and grab an interception in the same Super Bowl.

Who is the former player known as "Mean Joe"?

Joe Greene was the Defensive Rookie of the Year in 1969, and he went on to earn two Defensive Player of the Year awards as the cornerstone of the Pittsburgh Steelers' "Steel Curtain" defense, a unit that anchored four Super Bowl wins. Greene is just as well known for his nickname. "Mean Joe" captures his ferocity on the football field, but it became his calling card because his North Texas college team is called the Mean Green.

A lot of people remember Greene as the football player in the 1980 Super Bowl Coca-Cola commercial. In the ad, a boy offers a tired and limping Greene a Coke after he has walked off the field. Greene drinks the boy's beverage, then turns and tosses his jersey to the kid as a souvenir, saying, "Hey kid, catch!"

Super Stat:

25

The size of Perry's Super Bowl XX ring, the largest ever made and more than twice the size of the average male ring

Who was known as "The Fridge"?

William "Refrigerator" Perry was always big. He weighed 200 pounds as an 11-year-old, and was extremely athletic for his size — he could do a 360-degree dunk on a 10-foot hoop! Perry got his nickname at Clemson University. While bringing laundry back to his dorm room, teammate Ray Brown got into the elevator with Perry. There was barely any room between the two of them, so Brown said, "Man, you're about as big as a refrigerator." With that comment, a legend was born.

The Chicago Bears drafted Perry as a defender, but used him in short-yardage situations, too. He would block for Walter Payton, or bulldoze into the line himself for a first down or score. In Super Bowl XX, Perry scored on a 1-yard run in Chicago's 46–10 win.

Who looks like the superhero Thor because of his long blond hair?

It was an actor named Chris Hemsworth who played the role of the superhero Thor in the 2011 action movie called *Thor*, as well as in the 2012 flim, *The Avengers*. Had **Clay Matthews** not been playing outside linebacker for the Green Bay Packers at the time, his long golden locks, brute strength, and imposing attitude might've made him a strong candidate to play the part of the popular Marvel comics character.

Clay Matthews III is part of one of the most successful families of pro football players. His grandfather, Clay Sr., was a defensive lineman for the San Francisco 49ers in the 1950s. Clay III's father, Clay Jr., was a linebacker who played in three AFC Championship games for the Cleveland Browns during the 1980s. (Clay Jr. is also the oldest player to ever record a sack, doing so in 1986 at the age of 40 years and 282 days.) The most accomplished family member is Clay III's uncle, former offensive lineman Bruce Matthews. Bruce is a Hall of Famer who was named to the Pro Bowl more often (14 times) than any other offensive player in NFL history.

Clay III has certainly made his family proud since joining the NFL in 2009. He was named to the Pro Bowl after each of his first four NFL seasons, and he helped the Packers win Super Bowl XLV, in February 2011. He'll be a superhuman force for years to come.

DID YOU KNOW?

FAST FACT: Clay Matthews is the only NFL player to score a defensive touchdown and record at least 10 sacks in each of his first two seasons in the league.

The Matthews are the third family to produce three generations of NFL players. The NFL's first three-generation family happened in 1980 when Chicago Bears fullback Matt Suhey followed his father Steve, who played for the Pittsburgh Steelers, and his mother's father Bob Higgins, who was an end for the Canton Bulldogs. The Pynes later became the first family to have two genetic father-son relationships when Jim Pyne played for the Tampa Bay Buccaneers in 1995. Jim's father, George Pyne III, and grandfather, George Jr., had also been pro football players.

RECORD B

Players whose feats set the standards by

REAKERS

which future accomplishments are measured

Who has the record for most seasons with 100 or more receptions?

Denver Broncos receiver *Wes Welker* has made a career out of proving his doubters wrong. Despite a remarkable four-year stint during which he scored 90 touchdowns for Heritage Hall, a high school in Oklahoma City, Welker initially received no scholarship offers from colleges. College coaches felt that Welker's 5'9" frame would prevent him from succeeding against collegiate defenses. When his one and only scholarship offer from a Division I school did materialize, it came from Texas Tech University — a week after signing day. And that was only because projected signee Lenny Walls opted instead to attend Boston College.

Welker became a star at Texas Tech, where he set NCAA Division I records for punt return yards (1,761) and punt return touchdowns (eight). He also graduated as the school's all-time leader in catches (259) and receiving yards (3,069). Yet Welker ended up going unselected in the 2004 NFL Draft. The San Diego Chargers eventually did sign Welker, but then cut him after one game.

All of that seemed like ancient history when Welker caught a 12-yard pass for the New England Patriots against the San Francisco 49ers on December 16, 2012. It was his 100th catch of the year, marking the fifth time that Welker reached the century mark in receptions in one season. No other NFL player has ever done so.

Super Stat:

9

Number of times Welker has caught 12 or more passes in one game, which is more than any other player in NFL history

DID YOU KNOW?

FAST FACT: Despite playing only three seasons for the Miami Dolphins, Wes Welker is the team's all-time kickoff return leader with 3,756 yards.

Wes Welker caught the attention of the New England Patriots while playing for the AFC East rival Miami Dolphins. The first time he stood out was in a game at New England on October 10, 2004, when Welker filled in for injured Dolphins kicker Olindo Mare. He showed off his versatility by becoming the first NFL player with a kickoff return, punt return, field goal, extra point, and kickoff in the same game. The Patriots traded second- and seventh-round picks to Miami in exchange for Welker prior to the 2007 season.

Who has returned the most kicks for scores?

When it comes to returning kickoffs and punts, the Chicago Bears' *Devin Hester* is the greatest in NFL history. Hester broke the all-time record for most career return touchdowns on December 20, 2010, in only his fifth NFL season. His 64-yard return of a punt against the Minnesota Vikings was his 14th return TD in a regular-season game. It took Brian Mitchell 1,070 returns to reach the previous record of 13 career return touchdowns. Hester broke Mitchell's record on only the 286th return of his career.

FAST FACT: The 51st game-winning drive of Dan Marino's career came in his final victory, a 20-17 playoff win over the Seattle Seahawks on January 9, 2000.

Who has led his team on the most game-winning drives?

Dan Marino was at his best when it mattered most during his 17-year Hall of Fame career with the Miami Dolphins. Marino holds the NFL record for the most career game-winning drives in the fourth quarter or overtime with 51, including playoffs.

Marino's most famous game-winning drive was in 1994 against the New York Jets. The Dolphins had a first down at the Jets' 8-yard line with 30 seconds left when Marino motioned with his right arm as if he planned to spike the ball in order to stop the clock. The Jets relaxed. But right after the ball was snapped, Marino threw a pass to receiver Mark Ingram, who had run into the end zone, for a touchdown with 22 seconds remaining. The Dolphins won, 28–24.

Who has the most receiving yards in one post-season?

It didn't take **Larry Fitzgerald** long to become an NFL superstar. He led the league with 103 receptions in 2005 in only his second season. He was selected to play in the Pro Bowl seven times in his first nine seasons.

Fitzgerald's biggest accomplishment came in early 2009, after he helped lead the Arizona Cardinals to the playoffs for the first time in 10 years. Fitzgerald set records for most receptions, most receiving yards, and most touchdowns by a wide receiver in a single post-season. He caught 30 passes for 546 yards and seven touchdowns in only four games! Although the Cardinals fell short of winning the Super Bowl when they lost to the Pittsburgh Steelers, 27–23, Fitzgerald's performance is one that Arizona fans will surely never forget.

Super Stat:

8

Number of career touchdowns Fitzgerald has scored in the Pro Bowl, which is more than any other player

Who has the most sacks in one season?

In 2001, New York Giants defensive end *Michael Strahan* had at least part of a sack in every game, and he finished the year with an NFL record 22½ sacks. The record, however, did not come without controversy.

Strahan entered the final game of the regular season needing one sack to break the record held by the New York Jets' Mark Gastineau. Strahan still hadn't recorded a sack when the Green Bay Packers had the ball and a nine-point lead with less than three minutes remaining. Packers coaches called a running play, but quarterback Brett Favre instead rolled out as if he might pass. Favre ended up sliding into the feet of Strahan, who just had to fall on top of Favre to be credited with the sack that broke the record. Favre handed him the ball and several Giants came over to pat the quarterback on the head. "That was classy of Brett to do that," Giants tackle Lomas Brown said, referring to what he perceived as Favre's generosity on the play.

"I just react to what happens," Strahan said afterward. "What am I supposed to do? Get up and say, 'Brett! Why didn't you throw it?'"

Despite the controversy, Strahan was named 2001 NFL Defensive Player of the Year. He is likely to end up in the Pro Football Hall of Fame.

Super Stat:

2

Number of times Strahan led the NFL in sacks, in both 2001 and 2003

DID YOU KNOW?

FAST FACT: Michael Strahan is the New York Giants' all-time leader with 141½ career sacks, the fifth-highest total in NFL history.

Michasel Strahan has become a popular TV personality since his playing days ended after his New York Giants won Super Bowl XLII, in February 2008. Later that year, he joined former NFL stars Terry Bradshaw and Howie Long as a co-host on the *Fox NFL Sunday* pre-game show. In September 2012, Strahan was announced as Kelly Ripa's new co-host on the nationally syndicated morning talk show that had been called *Live! with Regis and Kelly,* when Regis Philbin had been co-hosting the show. The show then became known as *Live! with Kelly and Michael.*

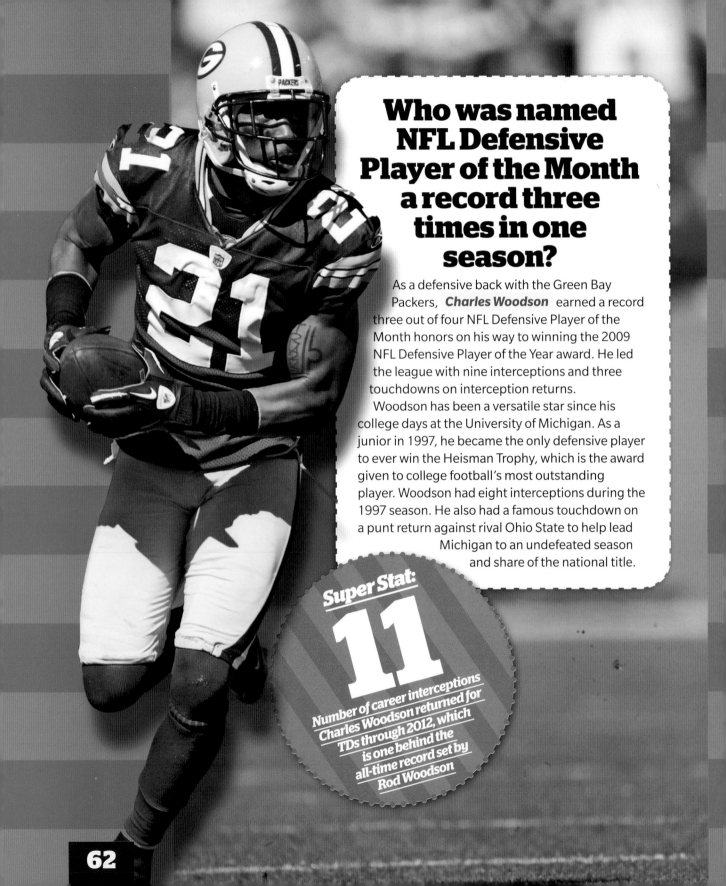

Who was named NFL Defensive Player of the Month a record three times in one season?

As a defensive back with the Green Bay Packers, *Charles Woodson* earned a record three out of four NFL Defensive Player of the Month honors on his way to winning the 2009 NFL Defensive Player of the Year award. He led the league with nine interceptions and three touchdowns on interception returns.

Woodson has been a versatile star since his college days at the University of Michigan. As a junior in 1997, he became the only defensive player to ever win the Heisman Trophy, which is the award given to college football's most outstanding player. Woodson had eight interceptions during the 1997 season. He also had a famous touchdown on a punt return against rival Ohio State to help lead Michigan to an undefeated season and share of the national title.

Super Stat:

11

Number of career interceptions Charles Woodson returned for TDs through 2012, which is one behind the all-time record set by Rod Woodson

Super Stat:

169

Number of consecutive passes Bradford threw without an interception at one point in 2010, which is an NFL rookie record

Who has the record for most completions by a rookie?

St. Louis Rams quarterback **Sam Bradford** completed 354 passes as a rookie in 2010, which shattered the previous record of 326 set by Peyton Manning in 1998. Bradford became the third rookie passer to start all 16 games and throw for more than 3,000 yards. He kept the Rams, who had a 1–15 record the previous season, in playoff contention until the final game of 2010.

An impressive debut season was nothing new for Bradford, who set the NCAA record for touchdown passes by a freshman with 36. As a sophomore at Oklahoma, he threw 50 TD passes and won the Heisman Trophy. Bradford was on his way to one of the best college careers ever before a shoulder injury limited him to three games as a junior. He was unable to throw for scouts prior to the 2010 NFL Draft, but the Rams still chose him with the first overall pick. He's proved plenty durable so far!

Who has the record for most sacks in one game?

Most of the 1970s and all of the '80s were a difficult time to be a fan of the Kansas City Chiefs: The team reached the NFL playoffs only once between 1972 and '89. It was no coincidence that the team's fortunes began to change soon after the arrival of linebacker **Derrick Thomas**.

Opposing NFL offenses took notice when Thomas was selected by the Chiefs with the fifth overall pick of the 1989 NFL Draft. It didn't take him long to emerge as an elite pass-rusher, at which point those same offenses began to dread playing against Kansas City. Thomas averaged nearly 12 sacks per season throughout the 1990s, and his stellar play was the foundation of a defensive unit that twice ranked as the NFL's best during that time. The Chiefs' defense was the key to Kansas City reaching the playoffs seven times that decade.

The best game of Thomas's Hall of Fame career came against the Seattle Seahawks on November 11, 1990. Pictured here is one of the seven times Thomas sacked Seattle quarterback Dave Krieg to break the single-game record of six sacks that Fred Dean had set with the San Francisco 49ers in 1983. Krieg managed to avoid yet another sack on the game's final play, when he dodged Thomas before throwing a touchdown pass for a 17–16 win.

Super Stat:

20

Number of sacks Thomas recorded in 1990; he's one of only nine players to reach that many sacks in one season

FAST FACT: Derrick Thomas was voted to the Pro Bowl in each of his first nine NFL seasons.

DID YOU KNOW?

Two players have come within one sack of Derrick Thomas's record since his seven-sack effort in 1990. One was the New York Giants' Osi Umenyiora, who had six sacks against the Philadephia Eagles on September 30, 2007. The other was Thomas himself, who had six sacks against the Oakland Raiders on September 6, 1998.

Who has the most receptions in a season?

Soft-spoken Indianapolis Colts wide receiver **Marvin Harrison** shattered an NFL record with 143 receptions in 2002. The record had been held by Detroit Lions wideout Herman Moore, who caught 123 passes in 1995. New England Patriots receiver Wes Welker tied Moore's mark in 2009, but no player has come within 20 receptions of Harrison! Harrison and quarterback Peyton Manning would spend many hours practicing together. Once the Colts broke the huddle, the two players trusted each other to be on the same page of the playbook, and they almost always were. The 953 completions, 12,756 yards, and 112 touchdowns on which they connected make Harrison and Manning the most prolific receiver–quarterback duo in NFL history.

Super Stat:

8

Number of consecutive seasons in which Harrison had 10 or more touchdown receptions, which is an NFL record

Super Stat:

7

The number of consecutive games in which Krause had at least one interception, an NFL record he set during his rookie season

Who has the record for most interceptions in an NFL career?

In 16 seasons with the Washington Redskins and Minnesota Vikings, safety **Paul Krause** intercepted a record 81 passes. He led the league with 12 interceptions as a rookie in 1964, which quickly established him as a master of anticipating passes and making big plays.

Krause was the original "centerfielder" defensive back. In fact, he had been an All-American centerfielder as a baseball player at the University of Iowa. Vikings head coach Bud Grant said about Krause, "Because he could read a quarterback as well as any defensive back I've known, he was able to record all of those interceptions."

Who holds the records for most post-season sacks in a career *and* in one game?

Willie McGinest was a key force on three Super Bowl-winning teams for the New England Patriots. He played linebacker as well as defensive end, and he seemed to save his best performances for the biggest games. In 17 career playoff contests, McGinest racked up a record 16 sacks. He set a single-game postseason record during the final playoff run of his career, with 4½ sacks in a 28–3 blowout of the Jacksonville Jaguars in a January 2005 playoff game.

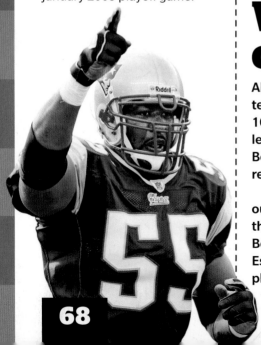

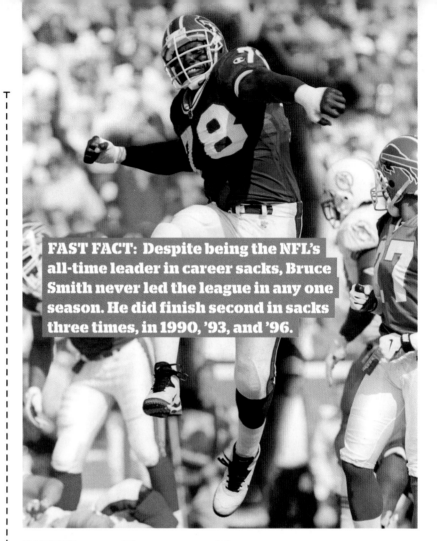

FAST FACT: Despite being the NFL's all-time leader in career sacks, Bruce Smith never led the league in any one season. He did finish second in sacks three times, in 1990, '93, and '96.

Who has the most career sacks?

Although NFL offensive linemen constantly double- and triple-teamed *Bruce Smith*, the Buffalo Bills defensive end recorded 10 or more sacks in a season 13 times. Smith is the NFL's all-time leader with 200 career sacks. He was selected to play in the Pro Bowl 11 times, and he was a key player on Buffalo teams that reached four straight Super Bowls in the early 1990s.

Smith had an elite combination of speed and size. He could outflank blockers, spin inside of them, or simply bulldoze right through them. One of Smith's hardest hits knocked Cincinnati Bengals quarterback Boomer Esiason out for four games. Still, Esiason said, "If I was a football coach and had Bruce Smith as my player, I would say to [young players], 'This is how you have to be.'"

Who has the rookie record for biggest touchdown-interception differential?

With 26 touchdown passes and only 10 interceptions in 2012, *Russell Wilson* of the Seattle Seahawks had one of the best seasons ever by a rookie quarterback. The undersized Wilson wasn't selected until the third round of the NFL Draft, but he went on to tie Peyton Manning's record for most touchdown passes by a rookie.

Many scouts believed that the 5'11" Wilson was too small to succeed — the average height of an NFL quarterback in 2012 was 6'3". Five quarterbacks and 69 other players were selected ahead of Wilson despite the fact that he set an FBS record for passing efficiency during his senior year at Wisconsin. His arm strength, intelligence, and running ability made up for his lack of height.

Wilson was a two-sport star in college who was twice drafted by Major League Baseball teams. He played 93 games between two minor-league teams in the Colorado Rockies' system before starting his NFL career.

Who has the record for the most consecutive completions?

As a star in college at Syracuse University, *Donovan McNabb* was a three-time Big East Conference Offensive Player of the Year. But because he succeeded as a dual-threat quarterback whose running ability often overshadowed his passing skills, many questioned whether he'd be able to run a pro offense. He was even booed by Philadelphia Eagles fans booed at the 1999 NFL Draft after the team selected McNabb with the second overall pick instead of running back Ricky Williams.

McNabb quickly established himself as one of the NFL's top passers. His best year was 2004, when he threw a career-high 31 touchdown passes with only eight interceptions while leading the Eagles to a 13–3 record. In Week 11 of that season, McNabb finished a 27–6 win over the New York Giants with 10 straight completions despite wind gusts of more than 20 miles per hour that day. He began the following week's game against the Green Bay Packers with 14 completions before one of his passes hit the ground. The 24 straight completions broke Joe Montana's record of 22, set in 1987. McNabb finished that day with a single-game team record 464 yards and a career-high five touchdowns.

Super Stat:
27
Number of times McNabb threw for 300 or more yards as a member of the Philadelphia Eagles, the most ever in team history

DID YOU KNOW?

FAST FACT: Mark Brunell completed 22 straight passes for the Washington Redskins in a 2006 game, which set the record for consecutive completions in *one game*. Six weeks later, David Carr of the Houston Texans tied Brunell's record.

One of the most memorable plays of Donovan McNabb's career came against the Green Bay Packers in a playoff game on January 11, 2004. Trailing 17–14 with just over one minute remaining in the fourth quarter, the Eagles needed 26 yards on a fourth-down play to keep their hopes alive. McNabb told receiver Freddie Mitchell, who hadn't caught a pass all day, to get ready. He then fired a pass to Mitchell over the middle of the field for 28 yards and the first down. The Eagles kicked a game-tying field goal seven plays later, then won the game in overtime.

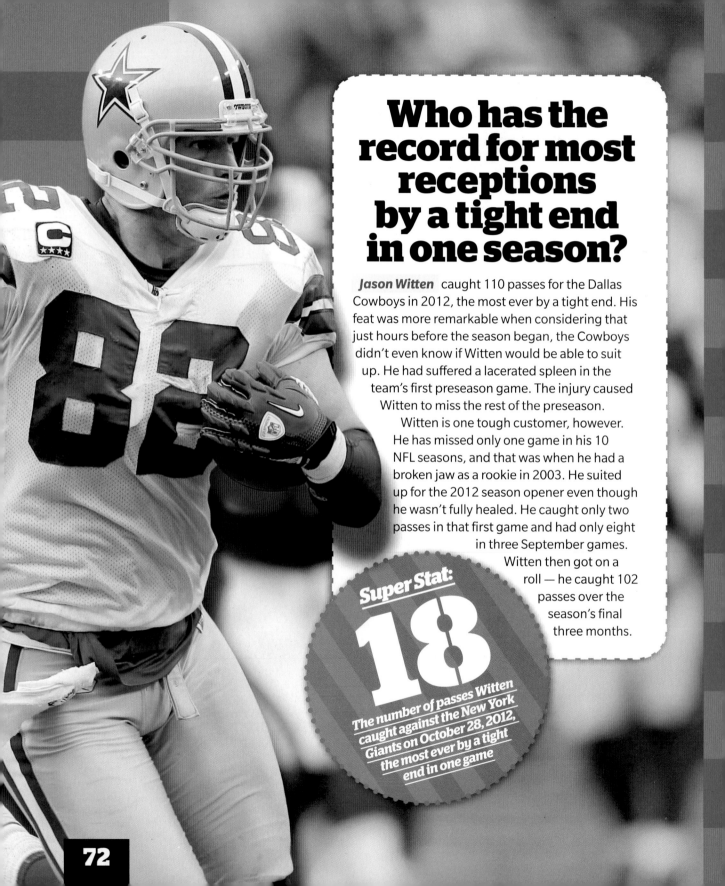

Who has the record for most receptions by a tight end in one season?

Jason Witten caught 110 passes for the Dallas Cowboys in 2012, the most ever by a tight end. His feat was more remarkable when considering that just hours before the season began, the Cowboys didn't even know if Witten would be able to suit up. He had suffered a lacerated spleen in the team's first preseason game. The injury caused Witten to miss the rest of the preseason.

Witten is one tough customer, however. He has missed only one game in his 10 NFL seasons, and that was when he had a broken jaw as a rookie in 2003. He suited up for the 2012 season opener even though he wasn't fully healed. He caught only two passes in that first game and had only eight in three September games. Witten then got on a roll — he caught 102 passes over the season's final three months.

Super Stat:

18

The number of passes Witten caught against the New York Giants on October 28, 2012, the most ever by a tight end in one game

Who has the most receptions in one game?

If you asked an NFL coach to design the perfect possession receiver, his image would likely resemble *Brandon Marshall*. A quick 6'4" wideout with the strength of a lineman, Marshall's aggressive after-the-catch running has made him the perfect target on short passes.

In Week 14 of the 2009 season, the Denver Broncos' offensive game plan was simple: Quarterback Kyle Orton throws to Marshall. Of the 28 passes Orton tossed his way, Marshall caught a record 21 of them for 200 yards. In response to the Indianapolis Colts' defensive scheme, Orton said, "You give me that matchup, and I'll take it 100 times out of 100 times." All told, Marshall accounted for more than half of his team's yards that day.

Super Stat:

4

The number of touchdowns Marshall scored in the Pro Bowl in January 2012, which set a new Pro Bowl record

Who has the record for longest overtime field goal?

The 57-yarder that *Sebastian Janikowski* of the Oakland Raiders kicked against the New York Jets in 2008 is the longest field goal ever made in overtime of an NFL game.

Janikowski was born in Poland, where his father played pro soccer. Sebastian became a soccer star, too, earning a spot on the Under-17 national team. He moved to the U.S. when he was 15 and joined his high school football team as a senior. He turned down contract offers to play pro soccer in South America, opting to attend Florida State, where he twice won the Lou Groza Award as the nation's best kicker. In 2000, the Raiders drafted Janikowski in the first round, the first time in 21 years that a kicker had been selected that early.

FAST FACT: Forced fumbles didn't become an official stat until 1991. Former defensive end Jason Taylor holds the career record with 47, which is only eight ahead of the 39 Charles Tillman had through the end of 2012.

Who has the record for most forced fumbles in one game?

Chicago Bears cornerback *Charles Tillman* has mastered the art of separating the football from offensive players. He does so by using a perfectly timed swipe of his fist, a move that has become known as the "Peanut Punch." "My aunt gave me the nickname when I was a little baby, and it just stuck," Tillman says of why he's called "Peanut." "I was a small kid growing up."

Tillman set an NFL record for most forced fumbles in a game, with four in a 51–20 win over the Tennessee Titans on November 4, 2012. Chicago's aggressive defense created more turnovers than any NFL team in 2012. "Peanut" finished the season with 10 forced fumbles, which tied an NFL record.

Who has won the most NFL Defensive Player of the Year awards?

Lawrence Taylor changed the NFL forever when he came into the league as a rookie in 1981. The linebacker terrorized opposing quarterbacks and was named NFL Defensive Player of the Year, an award he won again in 1982. The best season of his Hall of Fame career would come in 1986, when he had a career-high 20½ sacks. Taylor was named Defensive Player of the Year for a record third time, and he also earned the league's MVP award. His aggressive pass-rushing from the linebacker position set the tone for a future generation of sack specialists.

Who has the record for most career sacks by a linebacker?

I n 15 seasons with the Los Angeles Rams, Pittsburgh Steelers, Carolina Panthers, and San Francisco 49ers, *Kevin Greene* tallied 160 career sacks. That's the most ever by a linebacker, and it ranks third on the NFL's all-time list. The two players ahead of Greene, Bruce Smith and Reggie White, both played defensive end.

Greene was known for using his speed to explode around the edge of an offensive line to disrupt pass plays. He averaged more than a sack per game in back-to-back seasons, with 16½ in both 1988 and '89. Greene tallied the majority of his sacks during the 1990s, when he posted eight seasons of 10 or more sacks. He twice led the NFL in sacks, with 14 in 1994, and with 14½ in '96.

Greene was quite a character, known around the NFL for his enthusiastic play and zany personality. His long, flowing, blond hair gave him a distinctive look, especially when he was streaking past an offensive tackle to sack a quarterback. Greene was admittedly a "nutcake" and a "froot loop," who was often screaming, whooping, joking, and dancing on the field or sideline.

While nobody seemed to enjoy the physicality of the game more than Greene did, the fierceness on the field clearly wasn't enough. He even once joined the cast of WCW professional wrestling — the perfect fit for a guy who already looked a bit like legendary pro wrestling star Hulk Hogan!

Super Stat:

9

Number of consecutive games, starting on December 7, 1997, in which Greene had at least one sack, which is one shy of the NFL record

DID YOU KNOW?

FAST FACT: Kevin Greene ranks seventh all-time among NFL defensive players with 26 career fumble recoveries.

During off-seasons when he was an NFL player, Greene served as a captain in the United States Army Reserve. He traveled with fellow former NFL linebackers Lamar Lathon and Greg Biekert to visit U.S. troops in Iraq for a week in 2007. They went to boost the morale of soldiers and came home inspired by the bravery of men and women serving our country. "I told them all that they are the true heroes — my heroes," Greene wrote in a journal of the trip, which was published in the *Charlotte Observer*. "It was an unbelievable experience."

SUPER S

Their specialty is putting the ball either

CORERS

through the uprights or into the end zone

Who has the most rushing touchdowns by a quarterback in one season?

A lot was expected of *Cam Newton* when the Carolina Panthers selected the 6'5" quarterback with the first overall pick of the 2011 NFL Draft. Yet Newton still managed to exceed those high expectations with one of the most productive seasons ever for a rookie quarterback. He did it with both his arm and his legs. Newton became the first rookie in NFL history to throw for 4,000 passing yards, and he also scored 14 rushing touchdowns. It was the most rushing touchdowns ever by a quarterback in one season, breaking the record of 12 set by the New England Patriots' Steve Grogan in 1976.

Newton wasted no time making an impact in the NFL. In his first pro game, against the Arizona Cardinals, he threw for 422 yards. His total was 120 more than Peyton Manning's rookie record for most passing yards in a season's opening game! Newton proved that his performance was no fluke when, the following week, he threw for 432 yards against the defending Super Bowl champion Green Bay Packers. He became the first quarterback — rookie or not — to throw for as many as 854 yards through the first two games of an NFL season.

Newton had another impressive season in his second year, in 2012, with 3,869 passing yards, 19 passing touchdowns, and eight rushing TDs. His 7,920 passing yards are the most ever by a quarterback in his first two seasons. He also became the first player to reach both 30 passing TDs and 20 rushing TDs in just two NFL seasons.

DID YOU KNOW?

FAST FACT: Newton wore the Number 2 on his uniform at Auburn. He switched to Number 1 because another player, quarterback Jimmy Clausen, wore Number 2 for the Panthers when Newton was drafted by Carolina.

Not only did Cam Newton win the 2010 Heisman Trophy as college football's top player, but he also led his Auburn University Tigers to that season's national championship. He became the first player to win the Heisman, a national championship, and the NFL Rookie of the Year award.

Heisman Trophy

BCS National Championship

NFL Rookie of the Year award

Who is the youngest quarterback to throw five TD passes in one game?

Matthew Stafford of the Detroit Lions became the youngest quarterback to throw five touchdowns in a game when he did so in a dramatic 38–37 win over the Cleveland Browns on November 22, 2009. His fifth and final touchdown pass came on the game's final play, moments after a shoulder injury had forced Stafford to the sidelines. Lions head coach Jim Schwartz joked afterward that, "Matt's best play of the day might have been eluding four team doctors to get back on the field."

FAST FACT: Jacoby Jones had 56 receiving yards, 206 kickoff return yards, and 28 punt return yards in Super Bowl XLVII. His 290 all-purpose yards set a Super Bowl record.

Who has scored the longest touchdown in a Super Bowl?

Baltimore Ravens wide receiver and return specialist *Jacoby Jones* received the opening kickoff of the second half of Super Bowl XLVII eight yards deep in his own end zone. Many players would have taken a knee for a touchback to give their team the ball at their own 20-yard-line. Jones, however, raced up the middle of the field and barely had to break stride as he went 108 yards to the end zone. It was the longest play of any kind in Super Bowl history.

Jones's record-breaking return was his second long touchdown of the game. With less than two minutes to go before halftime, he fell down to haul in a long pass. Because he was untouched on the play, he scrambled to his feet before juking two San Francisco 49ers and finishing off a 56-yard score.

Who is the only player to rush for three touchdowns of more than 40 yards in the same game?

Many running backs have scored two long touchdown runs in one game. But only **Doug Martin** of the Tampa Bay Buccaneers has scored on three runs of at least 40 yards in a single contest. He did it on scampers of 45, 67, and 70 yards in a 42–32 win over the Oakland Raiders on November 4, 2012, and he did so while rushing for 251 yards. He joined former Denver Broncos running back Mike Anderson as the only NFL players to run for more than 250 yards and four scores in one game. Martin's performance helped earn him an invitation to the Pro Bowl after an oustanding rookie season.

Who has the record for touchdowns by a rookie?

Hall of Fame running back **_Gale Sayers_** scored 22 touchdowns during his rookie season with the Chicago Bears, in 1965. Known as the "Kansas Comet" because of the blazing speed he showed at the University of Kansas, Sayers was a hot prospect coming out of college. Both the Bears of the NFL and the Kansas City Chiefs, who were then part of the American Football League, selected him in the first round of their leagues' 1965 drafts.

Sayers also holds the career record for kickoff return average, with 30.6 yards per return. An injury to his right knee, and then one to his left knee two years later, limited his career to just 68 NFL games from 1965 to '71. Like a comet, he burned brilliantly for a short time.

Super Stat:

6

Number of touchdowns Sayers scored in one game in 1965, which tied an NFL record that hasn't been matched since

Super Stat:

60

Estimated speed in miles per hour at which the ball leaves Gronkowski's hand on one of his forceful spikes

Who has the most touchdowns by a tight end in one season?

The 18 touchdowns **Rob Gronkowski** scored in 2011 are the most ever for a tight end in one season. He set another tight end record with the 1,327 receiving yards he gained that year.

What the man known as "Gronk" has become most famous for, however, is his extremely hard spiking of the ball to celebrate a touchdown. "The Gronk Spike," as it has become known, debuted during the third game of the tight end's rookie season, in 2010. After catching a 5-yard touchdown pass against the Buffalo Bills, Gronkowski kicked up his left knee, hopped a few times on his right leg, and slammed the ball into the ground.

FAST FACT: Jason Taylor ranks sixth on the NFL's all-time list with 139½ career sacks.

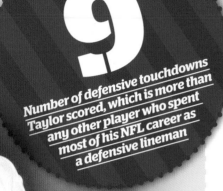

Super Stat:

9

Number of defensive touchdowns Taylor scored, which is more than any other player who spent most of his NFL career as a defensive lineman

Who has the most career touchdowns on fumble returns?

Throughout his 15-year NFL career, *Jason Taylor* was known as a disruptive force who consistently made game-changing plays on the defensive side of the ball. He was constantly around the action, whether dropping running backs behind the line of scrimmage or pulling down quarterbacks in the pocket. It was his relentless pursuit of the football that enabled Taylor to score six career touchdowns on fumble returns, which is the most in NFL history.

Taylor's best season was 2006, when he was named NFL Defensive Player of the Year as a defensive end for the Miami Dolphins. Not only did he set a career-high with nine forced fumbles, but he tied for the NFL lead with two touchdowns on interception returns. That's a remarkable achievement, considering it's a category almost always led by defensive backs.

DID YOU KNOW?

Taylor showed off his moves during a 2008 TV stint on *Dancing with the Stars*. He and his partner, ballroom dancer Edyta Sliwinska, finished in second place among the competition's 12 pairs. They were topped only by former Olympic figure skating gold medalist Kristi Yamaguchi and ballroom dancer Mark Ballas.

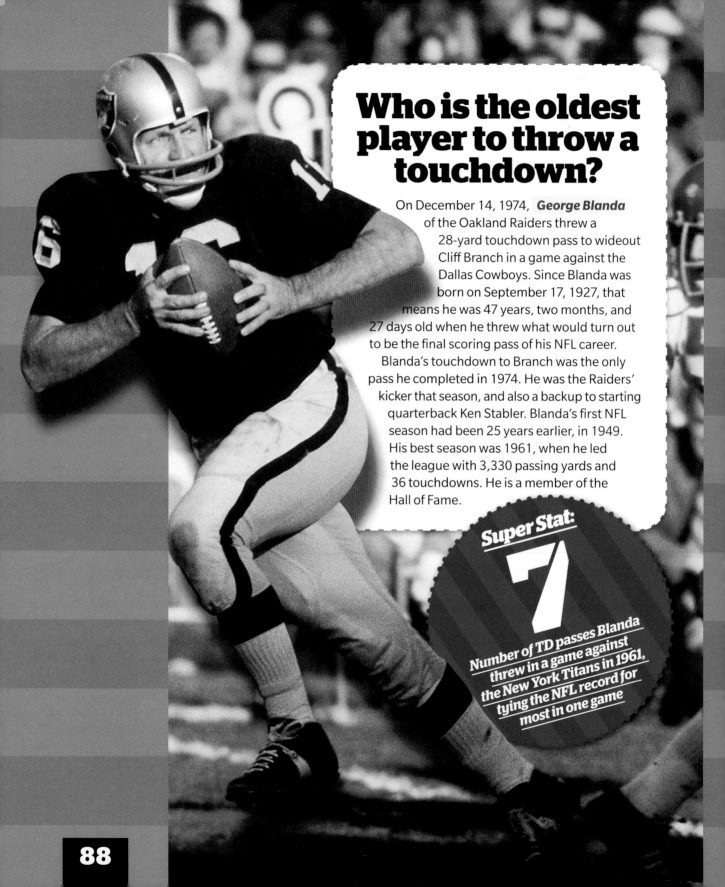

Who is the oldest player to throw a touchdown?

On December 14, 1974, **George Blanda** of the Oakland Raiders threw a 28-yard touchdown pass to wideout Cliff Branch in a game against the Dallas Cowboys. Since Blanda was born on September 17, 1927, that means he was 47 years, two months, and 27 days old when he threw what would turn out to be the final scoring pass of his NFL career. Blanda's touchdown to Branch was the only pass he completed in 1974. He was the Raiders' kicker that season, and also a backup to starting quarterback Ken Stabler. Blanda's first NFL season had been 25 years earlier, in 1949. His best season was 1961, when he led the league with 3,330 passing yards and 36 touchdowns. He is a member of the Hall of Fame.

Super Stat:

7

Number of TD passes Blanda threw in a game against the New York Titans in 1961, tying the NFL record for most in one game

Super Stat:

71

Number of passes Woodson intercepted in his career, which ranks third in NFL history

Who has the most TDs on interception returns?

Rod Woodson holds the NFL record for most career touchdowns on interception returns. The 1993 Defensive Player of the Year ran 12 picks back for scores during his Hall of Fame career.

Woodson went to Super Bowls as a member of three different teams: the Pittsburgh Steelers, Baltimore Ravens, and Oakland Raiders. After having spent the majority of his career at cornerback, Woodson moved to safety as a 34-year-old with the Ravens in 1999. He tied for the NFL lead that season in interceptions, with seven. The following season, he started all 16 games on a defense that led the Ravens to a Super Bowl victory. That defense is often named among the greatest defenses in NFL history.

FAST FACT: Four players share the NFL record for the longest field goal of 63 yards. The fourth one to do it was David Akers of the San Francisco 49ers in Green Bay on September 9, 2012.

Who holds the record for most field goals in one game?

On October 21, 2007, Tennessee Titans kicker *Rob Bironas* broke the record for field goals made in one game when he booted eight through the uprights against the Houston Texans. As it turned out, the Titans needed all eight of those kicks.

Tennessee starting quarterback Vince Young was sidelined that day. His backup, Kerry Collins, was having trouble leading the team to touchdowns once the Titans drove into Houston territory. Tennessee kept settling for field goal attempts. In the fourth quarter, the Texans scored 29 points and took the lead, 36–35, with 57 seconds left in regulation. But Collins moved the Titans into position for one last field goal. Bironas drilled a 29-yarder as time expired to give Tennessee a 38–36 win.

On the day, Bironas connected from 52, 43, 25, 21, 30, 28, 29, and 29 yards. The previous record of seven field goals in one game had been held by four different NFL kickers.

Super Stat:

35

Number of field goals Bironas made during the 2007 regular season, which was more than any other NFL kicker that year

DID YOU KNOW? Abilene Christian University's Ove Johansson kicked the longest field goal ever — in either college or pro — when he connected from 69 yards away on October 16, 1976. The kick came with 2:13 remaining in the first half of Abilene Christian's 17–0 victory over East Texas State.

Who completed the longest touchdown pass in overtime of a playoff game?

The 2011 Denver Broncos were in last place in the AFC West with a 1–4 record when they made **Tim Tebow** their starting quarterback over Kyle Orton. Tebow turned Denver's season around, leading the team to a division title. He did so more with his legs than his arm, finishing second among NFL quarterbacks in rushing yards, but just 32nd in passing yards.

It was Tebow's arm, however, that led Denver to a playoff win over the Pittsburgh Steelers. He threw for 316 yards, 80 of which came on a TD pass to Demaryius Thomas on the first play of overtime. It was the longest overtime TD pass in playoff history.

FAST FACT: The 35 field goals Blair Walsh made in 2012 matched the rookie record set by the New York Giants' Ali Haji-Sheikh in 1983.

Who has the most career points?

Morten Andersen scored a record 2,544 points over a 25-year NFL career with the New Orleans Saints, Atlanta Falcons, New York Giants, Kansas City Chiefs, and Minnesota Vikings. Andersen shares similarities with fellow kicker Gary Anderson, who is second in career scoring. Their names sound alike, and they both traveled to the U.S. as teens (Andersen from Denmark; Anderson from South Africa). In the NFC Championship game in 1999, Anderson missed a 38-yarder for the Vikings after not having missed all season. Andersen later made a 38-yarder in overtime for an Atlanta victory.

Who has the record for most field goals of 50 or more yards in one season?

Blair Walsh had one of the best seasons ever by an NFL kicker in only his first year in the league. As a rookie with the Minnesota Vikings in 2012, he successfully connected on all 10 of his field goal attempts from 50 yards or beyond. What a way to kick-start a career! The previous single-season record of eight field goals of 50 or more yards had been shared by Morten Andersen and Jason Hanson.

Even before his record-breaking 2012 season, Walsh was known for his powerful leg. His college team, the Georgia Bulldogs, plays in Athens, Georgia. Walsh was called the "Athens Assassin" for his ability to convert long field goal attempts.

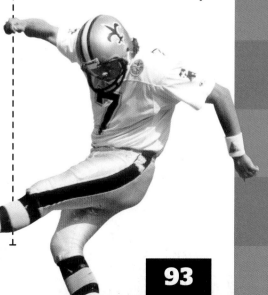

Who has scored the most touchdowns in NFL history?

On the first Monday Night game of the 1994 season, *Jerry Rice* of the San Francisco 49ers had a chance to break former Cleveland Browns running back Jim Brown's all-time NFL record of 126 career touchdowns. Rice had ended the 1993 season with 124 career TDs, so he needed two touchdowns to tie Brown, and three to break the record. Three touchdowns was a lot to expect in a game against a Los Angeles Raiders team that had made the playoffs the previous year and had the NFL's fifth-best pass defense in 1993. The Raiders had also improved their secondary from the previous year by signing cornerback Albert Lewis away from the Kansas City Chiefs.

Rice wasted little time reaching the end zone, giving the 49ers a 7–0 lead in the first quarter with a 69-yard touchdown catch from quarterback Steve Young. Rice would not score again until the fourth quarter, when his TD on a 23-yard run tied Brown's record and gave San Francisco a 37–14 lead that put the game out of reach. The only suspense left was whether Rice would be able to set a new NFL career touchdown record in front of his home crowd and a national television audience.

Sure enough, Rice outleaped Lewis for a 38-yard touchdown late in the fourth quarter. It was his third touchdown of the game and the 127th of his career. He would go on to score an astounding 81 more times to finish with 208 touchdowns, which is 33 more than any other player and 51 more than any other receiver. Many consider Rice to be the best player in NFL history.

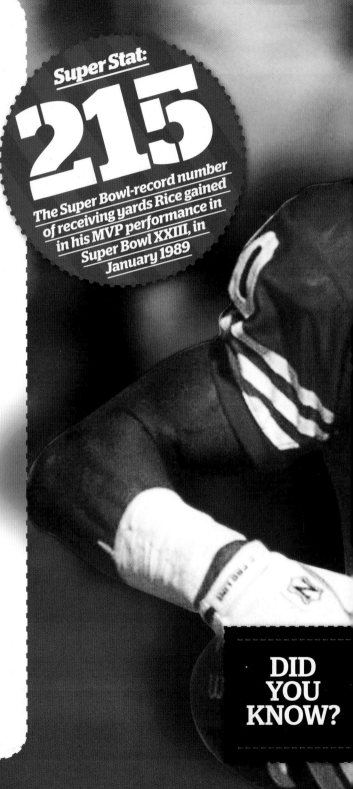

Super Stat:

215

The Super Bowl-record number of receiving yards Rice gained in his MVP performance in Super Bowl XXIII, in January 1989

DID YOU KNOW?

FAST FACT: Rice developed his reliable hands when he was a kid — he caught bricks on a scaffold while he assisted his father, who worked as a mason. Rice's pay was reduced for any bricks he would drop.

Jerry Rice played college football at a relatively small and obscure school called Mississippi Valley State University. It is a school that currently enrolls 2,500 students, which is more than the population of the city it's in, Itta Bena. Mississippi Valley State is part of the Football Championship Subdivision (FCS), which was known as Division I-AA when Rice played there from 1980 to '84. The honor awarded each season to the most outstanding freshman player in the Football Championship Subdivision is named the Jerry Rice Award.

Who has scored the most touchdowns in one NFL season?

LaDainian Tomlinson went on a rampage for the San Diego Chargers in 2006. The most impressive mark he set that year was the single-season touchdown record. It was the fourth time in seven seasons that the record had been broken.

In 2000, Marshall Faulk of the St. Louis Rams scored 26 times to break the record of 25 that had been set by the Dallas Cowboys' Emmitt Smith. Three years later, Kansas City Chiefs running back Priest Holmes reached the end zone 27 times, and Shaun Alexander of the Seattle Seahawks scored 28 times two years after that. Tomlinson topped them all, and he didn't do it by just one touchdown. His superhuman effort landed him three ahead of Alexander, with 31 touchdowns on the season. He also led the league in rushing yards that year, and won the NFL MVP award.

Super Stat:

38

Number of times Tomlinson rushed for two or more touchdowns in one game, the most of any player in NFL history

Super Stat:

1

Number of 99-yard TDs on rushing plays in NFL history, by Tony Dorsett of the Dallas Cowboys, on January 3, 1983

Who is the last player to score on a 99-yard touchdown reception?

In all, 13 NFL players have scored on the longest possible touchdown reception of 99 yards. The last one to do it was **Victor Cruz** of the New York Giants, in a game against the New York Jets on Christmas Eve in 2011. Cruz caught a pass from quarterback Eli Manning 10 yards beyond the line of scrimmage. He avoided tackle attempts by Jets defensive backs Antonio Cromartie and Kyle Wilson before taking off down the right sideline, where he outran Jets safety Eric Smith to the end zone.

Cruz was signed by the Giants after going undrafted in 2010. His break came early in 2011, when injuries to Giants wideouts Mario Manningham and Domenik Hixon thrust Cruz into a bigger role. He responded by setting a team record for most receiving yards in a season with 1,536.

Who has the most receiving touchdowns in a season?

Randy Moss may not be *the* best player ever at his position, as he claimed prior to Super Bowl XLVII when he told reporters, "I really think I'm the greatest receiver to ever play this game." But Moss is certainly *one of* the best. That was evident when he set an NFL single-season record with 23 touchdown receptions in 2007 as a member of the New England Patriots.

The Patriots went into their final game of the 2007 regular season with a perfect 15–0 record. When they trailed the New York Giants in the fourth quarter, 28–23, it seemed as if New England may fail to become the first team ever to end a season with a 16–0 record. That's when Moss caught a 65-yard bomb from quarterback Tom Brady. The touchdown put the Patriots ahead for good, helping to save their perfect season. The catch also gave Moss the record. He finished with one score more than the 22 Jerry Rice caught in 1987.

FAST FACT: Antonio Cromartie is the only player to pick off three Peyton Manning passes in one NFL game.

Who has kicked the longest field goal as a rookie?

In only the fourth game of his NFL career, *Greg Zuerlein* set a team record for the longest field goal ever by a Rams player. It was a 58-yarder in the first quarter of a September 30, 2012 game against the Seattle Seahawks. It turned out that his record would last less than two hours. That's because in the third quarter of the same game, Zuerlein topped himself by nailing a 60-yarder that is the longest field goal ever by an NFL rookie. His powerful leg has earned him a slew of nicknames, including "Greg the Leg" and "Legatron."

Who has scored the longest touchdown?

The Minnesota Vikings were trying to take a 10–7 lead into halftime of a 2007 game against the San Diego Chargers. So they sent in kicker Ryan Longwell to attempt a 57-yard field goal on the final play of the first half. What never occurred to the Vikings is that they might head into the locker room with a 14–7 *deficit*.

Longwell's kick came up short, and waiting for it at the back of the end zone was Chargers cornerback/kick returner *Antonio Cromartie*. He leaped to catch the ball without stepping out of bounds, and then started to return it. Cromartie raced up the right sideline, where he received a few blocks from his teammates. He would wind up going the entire 109-yard record distance for the score without even being touched by a Vikings player!

Who has the longest touchdown on an interception return?

There isn't much that safety **Ed Reed** can't do. Not only did he set the NFL record for the longest touchdown on an interception return when he went 108 yards against the Philadelphia Eagles on November 23, 2008, but the record he broke was his own! Reed had rambled 106 yards for the Baltimore Ravens on an interception return against the Cleveland Browns in 2004.

Because he studies film as hard as he plays, Reed learns about opposing teams' tendencies in the passing game. Combined with his ability to pick up on subtle signs that give away what a receiver and quarterback might do on a particular play, it makes Reed a master disruptor. He is the epitome of the label "ball hawk," often fooling quarterbacks into making what they think are safe throws in his direction. Once they do, his quick reflexes and body control enable him to bat passes away for incompletions, or to catch them for interceptions.

Reed became the all-time leader in interception return yards when he picked off a pass against the Cincinnati Bengals in the 2012 season opener and returned it 34 yards for a touchdown. He is the only player with more than 1,500 career interception return yards, and he is one of only 10 with more than 60 career interceptions.

FAST FACT: Ed Reed is the only NFL player to have returned a blocked punt, fumble, interception, and punt for touchdowns.

DID YOU KNOW?

When Ed Reed picked off a pass thrown by San Francisco 49ers quarterback Colin Kaepernick during the second quarter of Super Bowl XLVII, in February 2013, it was the ninth post-season interception of Reed's career. That tied him with three other players for the most post-season interceptions in NFL history.

YARDAG

The players who have excelled at moving

E KINGS

their teams up and down the field

Who has the record for most receiving yards in one season?

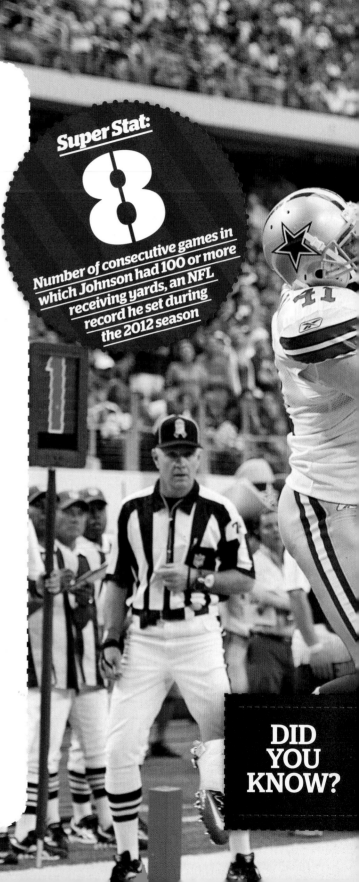

The Detroit Lions entered the 2007 NFL Draft having selected a wide receiver among the top 10 overall picks in three of the previous four drafts. So even though Georgia Tech wideout *Calvin Johnson* was considered one of the top talents coming out of college in 2007, many felt that the Lions might not risk using yet another high draft pick on a receiver. After all, both Charles Rogers (the second overall pick in 2003) and Mike Williams (the 10th overall pick in 2005) turned out to be busts.

The Lions ended up drafting Johnson, and Detroit fans are certainly glad they did. In only his second pro season, he tied for the NFL lead with 12 receiving touchdowns and ranked fifth with 1,331 receiving yards. In 2011, Johnson established himself as *the* best at his position, leading NFL wideouts with 1,681 yards and 16 touchdowns. He was even better in 2012, leading the league with 122 receptions and setting an NFL single-season record with 1,964 receiving yards, shattering Jerry Rice's previous mark of 1,848.

"Without a doubt, he's the best receiver in the league right now," Rice said in praising Johnson's peformance. He went on to predict that Johnson could end up as one of the best receivers to ever play the game. "The guy's gifted, but he also has the work ethic. He's only going to get better."

DID YOU KNOW?

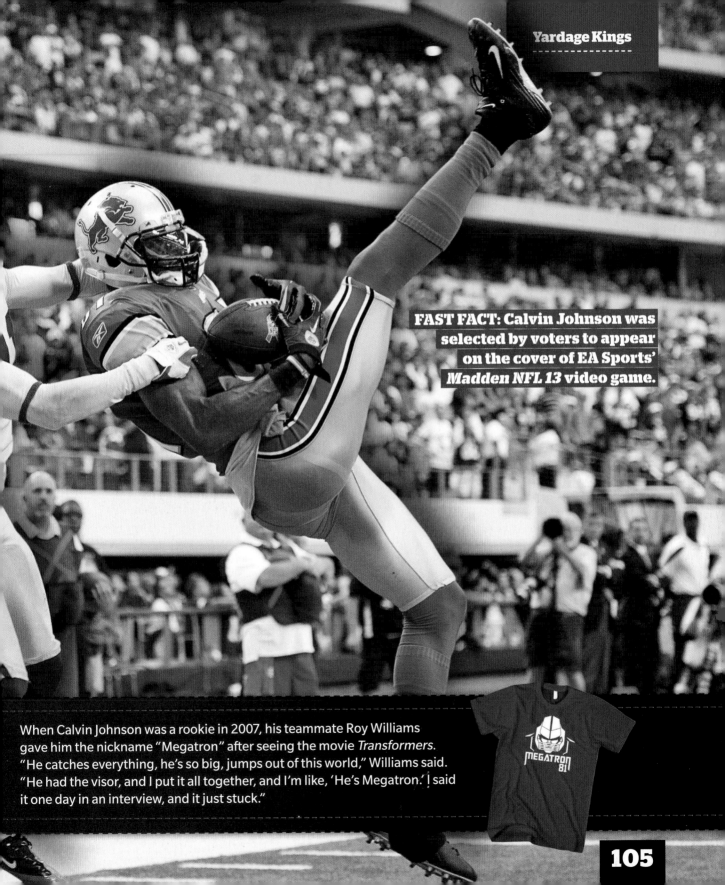

FAST FACT: Calvin Johnson was selected by voters to appear on the cover of EA Sports' *Madden NFL 13* video game.

When Calvin Johnson was a rookie in 2007, his teammate Roy Williams gave him the nickname "Megatron" after seeing the movie *Transformers*. "He catches everything, he's so big, jumps out of this world," Williams said. "He had the visor, and I put it all together, and I'm like, 'He's Megatron.' I said it one day in an interview, and it just stuck."

Who was the first quarterback to rush for 1,000 yards in a season?

Michael Vick did something in 2006 that no other quarterback had done before: He rushed for more than 1,000 yards in one season. Playing for the Atlanta Falcons, he gained 1,039 yards on 123 carries. That averages out to 8.45 yards per rush, which is an NFL single-season record, regardless of position. It broke a mark that had been set in 1934 by Chicago Bears running back Beattie Feathers. If you think that is impressive, consider this: As a quarterback, Vick has rushed for more career yards than Gale Sayers, who was one of the best *running backs* ever!

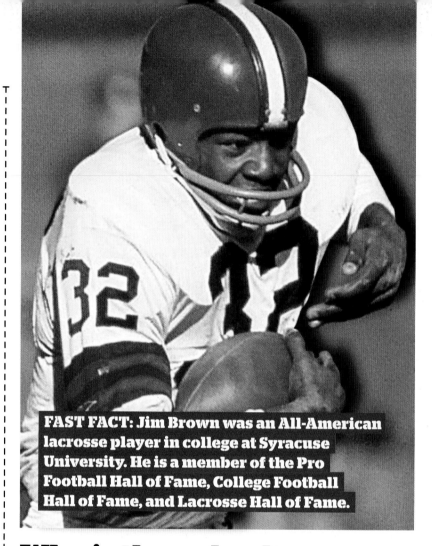

FAST FACT: Jim Brown was an All-American lacrosse player in college at Syracuse University. He is a member of the Pro Football Hall of Fame, College Football Hall of Fame, and Lacrosse Hall of Fame.

Who is the only player to lead the NFL in rushing for five straight seasons?

Few have ever moved the chains as effectively as *Jim Brown* did. The star running back spent his entire NFL career with the Cleveland Browns, and his bruising style helped him lead the league in rushing for five straight seasons, starting in 1957. After Jim Taylor of the Green Bay Packers took the title in 1962, Brown led the NFL again for another three straight years. He set a team record for most rushing yards in one season with 1,863 in 1963.

A book called *Football's Greatest*, which was published in 2012 by *Sports Illustrated*, ranked Brown as the best running back in NFL history. His career average of 104.3 yards per game is the highest mark of all time.

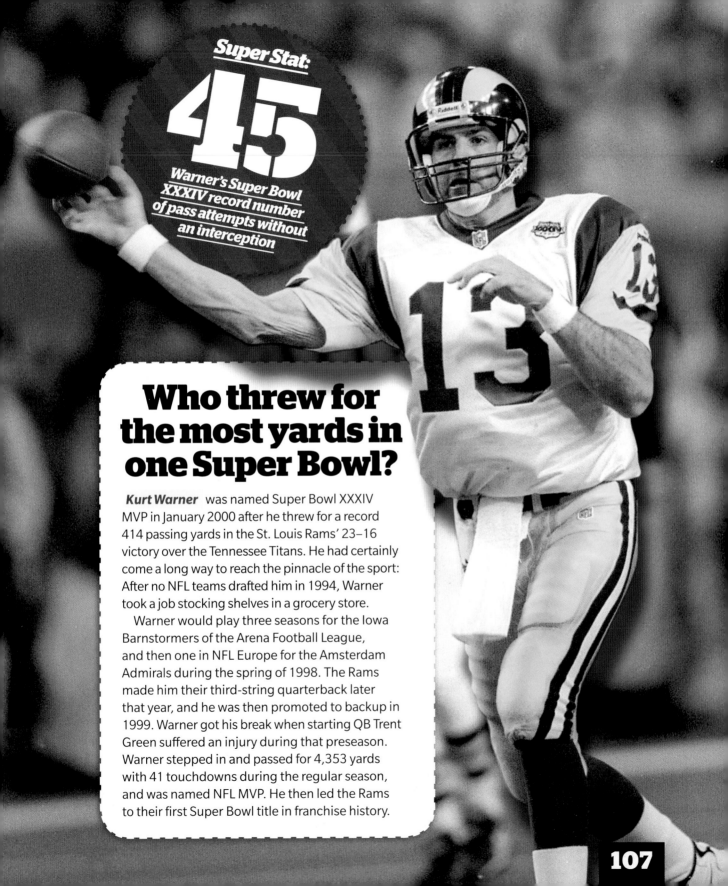

Who threw for the most yards in one Super Bowl?

Kurt Warner was named Super Bowl XXXIV MVP in January 2000 after he threw for a record 414 passing yards in the St. Louis Rams' 23–16 victory over the Tennessee Titans. He had certainly come a long way to reach the pinnacle of the sport: After no NFL teams drafted him in 1994, Warner took a job stocking shelves in a grocery store.

Warner would play three seasons for the Iowa Barnstormers of the Arena Football League, and then one in NFL Europe for the Amsterdam Admirals during the spring of 1998. The Rams made him their third-string quarterback later that year, and he was then promoted to backup in 1999. Warner got his break when starting QB Trent Green suffered an injury during that preseason. Warner stepped in and passed for 4,353 yards with 41 touchdowns during the regular season, and was named NFL MVP. He then led the Rams to their first Super Bowl title in franchise history.

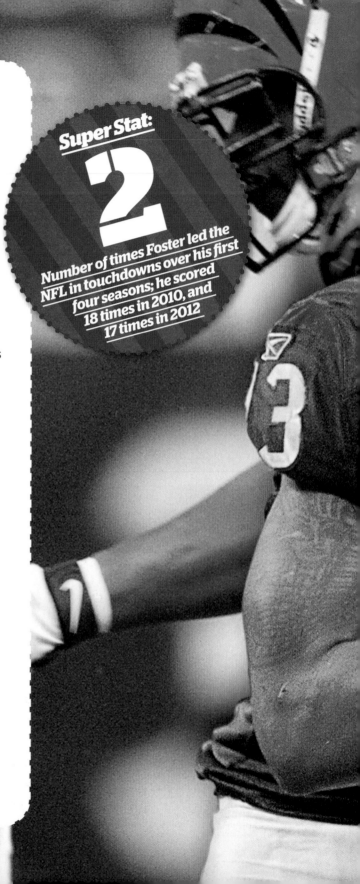

Who has the most yards from scrimmage in one season by an undrafted player?

People have been doubting Houston Texans running back *Arian Foster* for a long time. When he said in his seventh grade class that he wanted to grow up to become an NFL player, his teacher suggested that he should come up with a different answer. She thought it wasn't realistic for a kid to expect to become a professional football player.

"I took offense to that, because that's what I wanted to be," Foster says. "I want to inspire any kid out there . . . that if you really focus and you really put everything you have into it, you can do whatever you want to in this world."

Foster has gained a reputation for his intense workout regimen and strict diet, and both have paid off. Even though he ended his college career as the second-leading rusher in the history of the University of Tennessee with 2,964 yards, Foster did not get selected in the NFL Draft. He ended up spending most of 2009 on the Texans' practice squad. He then exploded onto the scene the following season, leading the NFL with 1,616 rushing yards. Foster also gained 604 receiving yards for a total of 2,220 yards from scrimmage, which broke Priest Holmes's single-season record for most yards from scrimmage ever by an undrafted player.

FAST FACT: Arian Foster is the only player ever to gain 100 or more rushing yards in each of his first three NFL post-season games.

DID YOU KNOW?

Arian Foster scored three touchdowns and set a single-game team record with 231 rushing yards in the Houston Texans' 34–24 victory over the Indianapolis Colts on September 12, 2010. He became the first player in league history to run for three touchdowns and more than 200 yards on the opening weekend of an NFL season.

Who has the most yards from scrimmage in a season?

Tennesse Titans running back **Chris Johnson** became the sixth player ever to rush for more than 2,000 in a season when he tallied 2,006 in 2009. He also gained 503 yards on 50 receptions, giving him an NFL single-season record of 2,509 yards from scrimmage. Johnson was named NFL Offensive Player of the Year for his efforts. With three TD runs of 85 or more yards in 2009 (91, 89, 85), he became the first player ever to register three *career* touchdown runs of 85 or more yards. No other NFL player had even one run of more than 80 yards in 2009.

Super Stat:

6

Number of touchdowns of 80 or more yards for which Johnson has run; no other player in NFL history has more than three

Who is the only player to rush for 1,500 or more yards in four straight NFL seasons?

Few, if any, NFL running backs have been as electrifying over a four-year period as **Barry Sanders** was for the Detroit Lions from 1994 to '97. He had consecutive seasons of 1,883, 1,500, 1,553, and 2,053 rushing yards to become the first player in league history with four straight years of at least 1,500 rushing yards.

Sanders is only 5' 8", but he made up for his lack of size with impressive leg strength and remarkable quickness. He was so elusive in the open field that defenders who tried to tackle him were often left lunging at air as Sanders raced in a different direction. Sanders was named NFL Offensive Player of the Year in both 1994 and '97.

Super Stat:

14

Number of consecutive games in which Sanders ran for 100 or more yards, an NFL record he set in 1997

Who is the running back with the most receiving yards in his NFL career?

The offense that was known as "The Greatest Show on Turf" would never have gotten the big top off the ground without one of the game's most versatile and productive players: *Marshall Faulk*. Faulk was traded from the Indianapolis Colts to the St. Louis Rams in 1999. That year, he teamed with quarterback Kurt Warner, and receivers Isaac Bruce and Torry Holt, to form one of the most potent offenses the NFL has ever known. The '99 Rams led the league with 526 points, which at the time was the third-highest total in NFL history. The 2000 Rams turned out to be even more explosive, leading the NFL with 540 points in 16 regular-season games.

One of the keys to St. Louis's aerial attack was Faulk's ability to make big plays as a receiver out of the backfield. He caught 80 or more passes for five straight seasons from 1998 to 2002. His 7-yard reception from Rams quarterback Ryan Fitzpatrick in the fourth quarter of a game against the Minnesota Vikings on December 11, 2005 broke the record Larry Centers had set for most career receiving yards by a running back.

Faulk ended his career after the 2005 season with 6,875 receiving yards. The first player in NFL history to gain 2,000 yards from scrimmage in four straight seasons (1998-2001), he retired as the ninth-ranked rusher of all time with 12,279 yards. In 2011, he was inducted into the Pro Football Hall of Fame.

DID YOU KNOW?

FAST FACT: The seven two-point conversions Marshall Faulk made during his career is an NFL record.

Marshall Faulk was held to only 17 rushing yards by the Tennessee Titans in Super Bowl XXXIV, in January 2000. He did catch five passes for 90 yards, and the Rams led by seven points when the Titans got the ball back for one last drive. Tennessee moved the ball to the St. Louis 10-yard line with six seconds remaining. On what would turn out to be the game's final play, quarterback Steve McNair completed a pass to receiver Kevin Dyson, who was tackled one yard short of the goal line by Rams linebacker Mike Jones as time expired. The Rams won the game, 23–16.

Who has the most all-purpose yards in one season?

When the New Orleans Saints signed **Darren Sproles** prior to the 2011 season, they knew they were getting a shifty runner capable of helping the team in a lot of ways. What nobody could've predicted was that Sproles would set an NFL record for most all-purpose yards in one season, in his first year with his new team. All-purpose yards includes those a player gets rushing and receiving, and also on kickoff and punt returns. Sproles rushed for a career-best 603 yards in 2011, and he gained 710 receiving yards on the 86 passes he caught from quarterback Drew Brees. Sproles finished second among NFL players in kickoff return yards with 1,089, and he gained 294 yards on punt returns for a total of 2,696 all-purpose yards. What a way to make a first impression on new teammates!

Super Stat:

66

Sproles's height, in inches, which made the 5' 6" running back the shortest player to gain a yard in an NFL game in 2011

Super Stat:

13

Number of times Gonzalez has been selected to play in the Pro Bowl, which is one shy of the NFL's all-time record

Who has the most career receiving yards for a tight end?

Tony Gonzalez is not only the greatest receiving tight end in NFL history, but his career numbers rank among those of the game's greatest wide receivers. He ended the 2012 season with 14,268 career receiving yards, which is by far the most ever by a tight end. It also ranks seventh among all players on the NFL's all-time list. The next tight end on the list is Shannon Sharpe, whose 10,060 career yards ranks 39th on that same list.

Gonzalez played basketball in college at the University of California, and he often uses the skills he developed on the hardwood to get an edge in the end zone. He'll sometimes use his size and strength to box out defensive backs, shielding them off with his body as if he's getting in position for a rebound. Other times, he'll outleap defenders to snatch the ball at its highest point. Those skills have helped Gonzalez become one of only six players in NFL history to catch more than 100 career touchdown passes.

Who has the most rushing yards in one game?

In only the eighth game of his NFL career, **Adrian Peterson** of the Minnesota Vikings ran around, over, and through the San Diego Chargers for three TDs and an NFL-record 296 rushing yards in a 33–17 win. Peterson racked up 253 of those yards after halftime, which is an NFL record for the most rushing yards in one half. Peterson nearly set another major NFL record in 2012, when he came up just nine yards short of breaking Eric Dickerson's single-season mark of 2,105 rushing yards. He did, however, win the 2012 NFL MVP Award.

FAST FACT: Andrew Luck's seven game-winning drives in the fourth quarter or overtime in 2012 were the most ever by a rookie quarterback.

Who has the most passing yards by a rookie?

When **Andrew Luck** was selected by the Indianapolis Colts with the first pick of the 2012 NFL Draft, he immediately had big shoes to fill. Peyton Manning had been the team's top overall pick in the 1998 draft, and was a star for many years. But Manning left the Colts and signed with the Denver Broncos a month prior to the 2012 draft.

Luck rewarded the Colts' confidence in him by leading them to an 11–5 record. He gave fans in Indianapolis an early Christmas gift by securing a 20–13 victory over the Kansas City Chiefs on December 23. The win clinched a spot in the playoffs with one game left in the season for a team that had gone 2–14 the previous year. In the game's second quarter, Luck broke Cam Newton's rookie record of 4,051 passing yards. Luck ended the season with 4,374 yards.

80

In 2012, Charles joined Barry Sanders and Chris Johnson as the only players with three runs of 80 or more yards in one season

Who has rushed for the most yards in one quarter?

Jamaal Charles rushed for more yards in the third quarter of a game against the New Orleans Saints on September 23, 2012 than some good running backs rush for in *two games*! His 162 yards in that quarter included a 91-yard touchdown that cut the Saints' lead to 24–13, and it sparked the Chiefs' impressive comeback. Kansas City would outscore New Orleans 11–0 in the fourth quarter and go on to win, 27–24, on a field goal in overtime.

The win over the Saints was one of the few highlights for the Chiefs in 2012. Kansas City tied the Jacksonville Jaguars for the worst record in the NFL at 2–14. Charles was the team's bright spot. He became the third Chiefs player to rush for more than 1,500 yards in one season. He also finished 2012 as the NFL's all-time leader for highest career rushing average by a running back with at least 750 attempts: His 4,536 yards on 784 carries equals 5.8 yards per carry. All-time great Jim Brown ranks second on the list at 5.2 yards per carry.

DID
YOU
KNOW?

Super Stat:

444

Kaepernick's number of combined yards (181 rushing, 263 passing) in his record-setting performance against the Packers, the most ever by a 49ers quarterback in a post-season game

Who has the most rushing yards by a quarterback in one game?

Many people questioned San Francisco 49ers head coach Jim Harbaugh's decision to replace starting quarterback Alex Smith with backup *Colin Kaepernick* in the middle of the 2012 regular season. After all, Smith had led the 49ers to the NFC Championship Game after the 2011 season.

The gamble paid off. In the first post-season start of his career, Kaepernick led the 49ers to a 45–31 win over the Green Bay Packers. His 181 rushing yards in that game set an NFL record for quarterbacks, in the regular season or playoffs. It topped the previous mark of 173 yards set by Michael Vick on December 1, 2002.

Not only is Colin Kaepernick an oustanding athlete, but he also seems to have an ability to predict the future! When he was in fourth grade, he wrote a letter to himself. In it, he predicted that he would grow to be between 6' and 6' 4" tall, and that he would "then go to the pros and play on the Niners or Packers even if they aren't good in seven years."

Colin

I'm 5ft 2inches 91 pounds. Good N athletc. I think in 7 years I will be between 6ft - to 6ft 4inches 140 pounds. I hope I go to a good colleye in falk Then go to the pros and play on the niners or the packers even If they wren't good in seven years, My Friend are Jason, kyler, leo, Spencer, Mark and Jacob.

Sincerly
Colin

Who has the record for most seasons with 4,000 or more passing yards?

When **Peyton Manning** missed the entire 2011 season after having to undergo four neck surgeries, many questioned whether he would ever be as great as he had been for the Indianapolis Colts. The Denver Broncos had no such doubts, signing Manning to a five-year contract once the Colts released him after the 2011 season.

Manning led the Broncos to a 13–3 record in 2012 and a first-place finish in the AFC West. He threw for 4,659 yards to extend his NFL record to 12 career 4,000-yard seasons. He led the league with a completion percentage of 68.6 and was named NFL Comeback Player of the Year.

"I feel very, very privileged to be back playing football again," Manning said after accepting the award. "After not playing for a year, I certainly missed being out there with my teammates, being out there playing the game that I love."

Who has the most rushing yards in one season?

When the Rams were still in Los Angeles, they were known for one thing: *Eric Dickerson* . The tall tailback with the upright running style was practically his team's entire offense. His long strides and straight-line speed enabled him to glide by defenders, who took bad angles trying to tackle him. They constantly misjudged Dickerson's speed.

In 1984, Dickerson had a remarkable season. His 2,105 yards rushing set the NFL's single-season record. He surpassed 200 yards twice and 140 yards in a game seven times. Minnesota Vikings running back Adrian Peterson came close to Dickerson's record in 2012, but Peterson's 2,097-yard effort came up eight yards short of the mark. Close, but no cigar.

Super Stat:

18

Number of touchdowns Dickerson rushed for as a rookie in 1983, the most rushing touchdowns ever by a rookie

Who has the most interception return yards in one NFL season?

A lot of NFL teams thought **Darren Sharper** was washed up after he intercepted only one pass in 16 games in 2008. It was his 12th NFL season, and when it was over, his Minnesota Vikings did not renew his contract. That left Sharper to sign with the New Orleans Saints prior to the 2009 season.

As it turned out, Sharper was far from washed up. He tied for the NFL lead in 2009 in both interceptions, with nine, and interceptions returned for touchdowns, with three. Two of his TDs were on interception returns of more than 90 yards. The first one was a 95-yard return against the Philadelphia Eagles on September 20. His 99-yard return against the New York Jets two weeks later was the longest in Saints team history. And when Sharper returned an interception 21 yards against the Tampa Bay Buccaneers on December 27, it gave him 376 interception return yards for the season, which set a new NFL record.

FAST FACT: Roger Craig's 92 receptions in 1985 led all NFL players. He remains the only running back ever to lead the NFL in receptions for a single season.

Who was first to reach 1,000 rushing and 1,000 receiving yards in one NFL season?

" *Roger Craig* is going to become a great football player very soon," San Francisco 49ers head coach Bill Walsh said during the summer of 1983. At the time, Craig was in his first training camp with the team after being a second-round pick in the NFL Draft. In 1984, Craig led the 49ers with 71 receptions even though he was a running back. He ended the season by becoming the first player ever to score three touchdowns in a Super Bowl, which he did during the 49ers' 38–16 win over the Miami Dolphins. The following year, Craig became the first player ever to reach 1,000 rushing yards and 1,000 receiving yards in the same NFL season. His head coach sure called that one!

Who has the NFL record for most career passing yards?

Brett Favre holds many of the NFL's most important career passing records. Among those records is the 71,838 passing yards he amassed over 16 seasons with the Green Bay Packers, one with the New York Jets, and two with the Minnesota Vikings. Dan Marino, who ranks second in career passing yards, is more than 10,000 yards behind Favre. Durability was a key reason Favre was able to rack up such an impressive total. He set an NFL record by starting 297 straight regular-season games between September 1992 and December 2010.

FAST FACT: By having "GRIFFIN III" on his jersey, Robert Griffin III became the first player in any of the four major U.S. pro sports leagues — NFL, MLB, NBA or NHL — to wear Roman numerals on his back.

DID YOU KNOW?

Super Stat:

37

Number of years the Redskins had gone without an Offensive Rookie of the Year between Mike Thomas in 1975 and Robert Griffin III in 2012

Who has the most rushing yards by a rookie QB?

With 45 seconds left in the third quarter of a game against the New York Giants on December 3, 2012, *Robert Griffin III* ran around the left end of the line for seven yards to the 50-yard line. That gave him 707 rushing yards for the season, which broke Cam Newton's record for rushing yards by a rookie quarterback. Remarkably, Griffin's Washington Redskins had more than 17 quarters left to play in the season!

Griffin ended up with 815 rushing yards even though he had to miss one of the team's remaining games because of a knee injury. He became the fourth quarterback — rookie of not — ever to surpass 800 rushing yards in a season, joining Randall Cunningham, Michael Vick, and Bobby Douglas. Griffin threw 20 touchdown passes and only five interceptions while leading the Redskins to a 10–6 record and their first NFC East division title since 1999.

Robert Griffin III was the 27th NFL Offensive Rookie of the Year from an NFC team since the award was first given out in 1967. The NFC's Minnesota Vikings have had five players win the award, which is more than any team in the NFL. These four NFC teams have never had an Offensive Rookie of the Year:

New York Giants

Philadelphia Eagles

San Francisco 49ers

Seattle Seahawks

Player Index

Super Stat:

37

Number of years the Redskins had gone without an Offensive Rookie of the Year between Mike Thomas in 1975 and Robert Griffin III in 2012

Who has the most rushing yards by a rookie QB?

With 45 seconds left in the third quarter of a game against the New York Giants on December 3, 2012, *Robert Griffin III* ran around the left end of the line for seven yards to the 50-yard line. That gave him 707 rushing yards for the season, which broke Cam Newton's record for rushing yards by a rookie quarterback. Remarkably, Griffin's Washington Redskins had more than 17 quarters left to play in the season!

Griffin ended up with 815 rushing yards even though he had to miss one of the team's remaining games because of a knee injury. He became the fourth quarterback — rookie of not — ever to surpass 800 rushing yards in a season, joining Randall Cunningham, Michael Vick, and Bobby Douglas. Griffin threw 20 touchdown passes and only five interceptions while leading the Redskins to a 10–6 record and their first NFC East division title since 1999.

Robert Griffin III was the 27th NFL Offensive Rookie of the Year from an NFC team since the award was first given out in 1967. The NFC's Minnesota Vikings have had five players win the award, which is more than any team in the NFL. These four NFC teams have never had an Offensive Rookie of the Year:

New York Giants

Philadelphia Eagles

San Francisco 49ers

Seattle Seahawks

Player Index

A

Allen, Jared, 36-37
Andersen, Morten, 79, 93

B

Bettis, Jerome, 31, 35
Bironas, Rob, 90-91
Blanda, George, 78, 88
Bradford, Sam, 63
Bradshaw, Terry, 13
Brady, Tom, 26-27
Brees, Drew, 4, 6-7
Brown, Jim, 102, 106

C

Carson, Harry, 30, 44
Charles, Jamaal, 117
Collinsworth, Cris, 39
Craig, Roger, 123
Cromartie, Antonio, 78, 99
Cruz, Victor, 79, 97

D

Dalton, Andy, 50
Davis, Terrell, 17
Dickerson, Eric, 121

E

Elway, John, 18-19
Esiason, Boomer, 34

F

Faulk, Marshall, 112-113
Favre, Brett, 123
Fitzgerald, Larry, 54, 59
Flacco, Joe, 22-23
Foster, Arian, 103, 108-109

G

Gastineau, Mark, 34
Gonzalez, Tony, 115
Graham, Otto, 10-11
Greene, Joe, 50
Greene, Kevin, 76-77
Griffin III, Robert, 103, 124-125
Gronkowski, Rob, 78, 85

H

Haley, Charles, 9
Harrison, James, 4, 25
Harrison, Marvin, 66
Hester, Devin, 54, 58
Holmes, Santonio, 21

Howard, Desmond, 20

J

Janikowski, Sebastian, 74
Johnson, Calvin, 103, 104-105
Johnson, Chad, 30, 48
Johnson, Chris, 110
Jones-Drew, Maurice, 32-33
Jones, Jacoby, 82

K

Kaepernick, Colin, 118-119
Krause, Paul, 67

L

Lewis, Ray, 5, 29
Luck, Andrew, 102, 116

M

Manning, Eli, 4, 8
Manning, Peyton, 102, 120
Marino, Dan, 54, 58
Marshall, Brandon, 55, 73

Photo Credits

Cover: Illustration by Artistic Image / AA Reps Inc.

Front Cover: Simon Bruty (Eli Manning); Rob Shanahan / WireImage.com (Emmitt Smith); Andy Hayt (Joe Montana)

Back Cover: Robert Beck (Peyton Manning); John Biever (Rod Woodson); Simon Bruty (Robert Griffin III); David E. Klutho (Darren Sproles)

Page 4: John Biever (Eli Manning, James Harrison), Robert Beck (Drew Brees), Andy Hayt (Joe Montana)

Page 5: Damon Strohmeyer (Aaron Rodgers), Neil Leifer (Joe Namath), Bob Rosato (Adam Vinatieri), Al Tielemans (Ray Lewis, Emmitt Smith)

Pages 6-7: Robert Beck

Page 8: Neil Leifer (Bart Starr), John Biever (Eli Manning)

Page 9: George Tiedemann

Pages 10-11: Evan Peskin

Page 12: Andy Hayt

Page 13: Neil Leifer

Pages 14-15: Damian Strohmeyer

Page 16: Andy Hayt

Page 17: Al Tielemans (Emmitt Smith), John Iacono (Terrell Davis)

Pages 18-19: Bob Rosato

Page 20: John Biever

Page 21: Peter Read Miller

Pages 22-23: Al Tielemans

Page 24: Bob Rosato (Adam Vinatieri), Al Tielemans (Steve Young)

Page 25: John Biever

Pages 26-27: Bob Rosato

Page 28: Neil Leifer

Page 29: Al Tielemans

Page 30: Jerry Wachter (Harry Carson), Al Tielemans (Terrell Owens), Damian Strohmeyer (Chad Johnson), Allen Kee / Getty Images (John Randle)

Page 31: John W. McDonough (Darrelle Revis), Glenn James / WireImage.com (Deion Sanders), Al Tielemans (Jerome Bettis), Heinz Kluetmeier (Walter Payton), Thomas B. Shea / Getty Images (J.J. Watt)

Pages 32-33: Damian Strohmeyer

Page 34: Andy Hayt (Boomer Esiason), Jerry Wachter (Mark Gastineau)

Page 35: John Iacono

Pages 36-37: John Biever

Page 38: Heinz Kluetmeier

Page 39: Focus on Sport / Getty Images

Pages 40-41: Glenn James / WireImage.com

Page 42: John W. McDonough

Page 43: Al Tielemans

Page 44: Jerry Wachter

Page 45: Allen Kee / Getty Images (John Randle), Al Tielemans (Troy Polamalu)

Pages 46-47: Peter Read Miller

Page 48: Damian Strohmeyer

Page 49: Thomas B. Shea / Getty Images

Page 50: John Biever (Andy Dalton), Neil Leifer (Joe Greene)

Page 51: Bill Smith / Getty Images

Pages 52-53: John Biever

Page 54: Peter Read Miller

Page 54: Mickey Pfleger (Dan Marino), Simon Bruty (Larry Fitzgerald), Rob Carr / Getty Images (Jason Witten), Rick Stewart / Getty Images (Bruce Smith)

Page 55: Al Tielemans (Brandon Marshall, Michael Strahan, Willie McGinest), John W. McDonough (Russell Wilson), John Biever (Charles Woodson)

Pages 56-57: Simon Bruty

Page 58: Peter Read Miller (Devin Hester), Mickey Pfleger (Dan Marino)

Page 59: Simon Bruty

Pages 60-61: Al Tielemans

Page 62: John Biever

Page 63: Simon Bruty

Pages 64-65: John Biever

Page 66: John Biever

Page 67: Tony Tomsic / Getty Images

Page 68: Al Tielemans (Willie McGinest), Rick Stewart / Getty Images (Bruce Smith)

Page 69: John W. McDonough

Pages 70-71: Damian Strohmeyer

Page 72: Rob Carr / Getty Images

Page 73: Al Tielemans

Page 74: Jed Jacobsohn / Getty Images

Page 75: Simon Bruty (Charles Tillman), Peter Read Miller (Lawrence Taylor)

Pages 76-77: Damian Strohmeyer

Page 78: George Long / Getty Images (George Blanda), Peter Read Miller (Antonio Cromartie), David E. Klutho (Matthew Stafford), Damian Strohmeyer (Rob Gronkowski), Simon Bruty (Cam Newton)

Page 79: Erza Shaw / Getty Images (Doug Martin), John W. McDonough (Jerry Rice), John Biever (Rod Woodson), Focus on Sport / Getty Images (Morten Andersen), Rob Tringali / SportsChrome / Getty Images (Victor Cruz)

Pages 80-81: Simon Bruty

Page 82: David E. Klutho (Matthew Stafford), Al Tielemans (Jacoby Jones)

Page 83: Erza Shaw / Getty Images

Page 84: Focus on Sport / Getty Images

Page 85: Damian Strohmeyer

Pages 86-87: Bill Frakes

Page 88: George Long / Getty Images

Page 89: John Biever

Pages 90-91: Jamie Squire / Getty Images (Rob Bironas), Mark Elmore (Ove Johansson)

Page 92: Robert Beck

Page 93: Patric Schneider / AP (Blair Walsh), Focus on Sport / Getty Images (Morten Andersen)

Pages 94-95: John W. McDonough

Page 96: Robert Beck

Page 97: Rob Tringali / SportsChrome / Getty Images

Page 98: Bob Rosato

Page 99: Peter Read Miller (Antonio Cromartie) Dilip Vishwanat / Getty Images (Greg Zuerlein)

Pages 100-101: Jim McIsaac / Getty Images

Page 102: Neil Leifer (Jim Brown), Simon Bruty (Andrew Luck), Doug Pensinger / Getty Images (Adrian Peterson), Robert Beck (Peyton Manning)

Page 103: Simon Bruty (Robert Griffin III), David E. Klutho (Darren Sproles, Calvin Johnson), John Biever (Arian Foster)

Pages 104-105: David E. Klutho

Page 106: Simon Bruty (Michael Vick), Neil Leifer (Jim Brown)

Page 107: Peter Read Miller

Pages 108-109: John Biever

Page 110: Bill Frakes

Page 111: Andy Hayt / Getty Images

Pages 112-113: John Biever

Page 114: David E. Klutho

Page 115: Bob Rosato

Page 116: Doug Pensinger / Getty Images (Adrian Peterson), Simon Bruty (Andrew Luck)

Page 117: David Eulitt / Kansas City Star / MCT via Getty Images

Pages 118-119: John W. McDonough

Page 120: Robert Beck

Page 121: Peter Brouillet / Getty Images

Page 122: Simon Bruty

Page 123: George Rose / Getty Images (Roger Craig) John Biever (Brett Favre)

Pages 124-125: Simon Bruty